Lessons from the Life of Moses

Lessons from the Life of Moses

Lance Lambert

LANCE LAMBERT MINISTRIES

Richmond, VA

ISBN: 978-1-68389-080-5
www.lancelambert.org

Contents

Preface

The messages contained in this booklet were given by Lance Lambert in July 1993 at the Western Christian Conference. They have been transcribed and printed by permission with minimal editing for clarity. The printed messages have not been reviewed by the speaker. Unless otherwise indicated, all Scripture quotations are from the American Standard Version of the Bible (1901).

1.
The Man of God

Deuteronomy 33:1

And this is the blessing, wherewith Moses the man of God blessed the children of Israel before his death.

Deuteronomy 34:5, 10

So Moses the servant of the Lord died there in the land of Moab, according to the word of the Lord. And there hath not arisen a prophet since in Israel like unto Moses, whom the Lord knew face to face.

Acts 7:17–29

But as the time of the promise drew nigh which God vouchsafed unto Abraham, the people grew and multiplied in Egypt, till there arose another king over Egypt, who knew not Joseph. The same dealt craftily with our race, and ill-treated our fathers, that they should cast out their babes to the end they might not live. At which season Moses was born, and was exceeding fair; and he was nourished three months in his father's house: and when he was cast out, Pharaoh's daughter took him up, and nourished him for her own son. And Moses was instructed in all the wisdom of the Egyptians; and he was mighty in his words and works. But when he was well-nigh forty years old, it came into his heart to visit his brethren the children of Israel. And seeing one of them suffer wrong, he defended him, and avenged him that was oppressed, smiting the Egyptian: and he supposed that his brethren understood that God by his hand was giving them deliverance; but they understood not. And the day following he appeared unto them as they strove, and would have set them at one again, saying, Sirs, ye are brethren; why do ye wrong one to another? But he that did his neighbor wrong thrust him away, saying, Who made thee a ruler and a judge over us? Wouldest thou kill me, as thou killedst the Egyptian yesterday? And Moses fled at this saying, and became a sojourner in the land of Midian, where he begat two sons.

Hebrews 11:23–27

By faith Moses, when he was born, was hid three months by his parents, because they saw he was a goodly child; and they were not afraid of the king's commandment. By faith Moses, when he was grown up, refused to be called the son of Pharaoh's daughter; choosing rather to share ill treatment with the people of God, than to enjoy the pleasures of sin for a season; accounting the reproach of Christ greater riches than the treasures of Egypt: for he looked unto the recompense of reward. By faith he forsook Egypt, not fearing the wrath of the king: for he endured, as seeing him who is invisible.

These are lessons from the life of Moses, and they are all to do with spiritual character and service. Of course, I do not have to tell you that Moses is one of the greatest characters in the Old Testament, indeed in the Bible. It is very interesting that there are only two that have been selected to represent all God's dealings and all His work amongst His own under the old covenant, and those two are Moses and Elijah. You will remember when the Lord Jesus was transfigured in glory, it was Moses and Elijah who were seen sharing and talking with Him about His exodus. Interestingly, the word *decease* in the old version is "exodus" in Greek; it is His "exit." Moses and Elijah both talked to the Lord Jesus about His exodus. I sometimes wish that we had been there and heard a little of that extraordinary discussion that the Lord Jesus had with Moses and Elijah on that Mount of Transfiguration.

In the letter of the apostle Paul to the Corinthians Paul says, "Now these things happened unto them by way of example; and they were written for our admonition [instruction], upon whom the ends of the ages are come" (1 Corinthians 10:11).

So we have an understanding from the New Testament that all God's dealings with Moses, as indeed with the others, were for our instruction upon whom the ends of the ages have come. Moses is described in three ways. He is described as the man of God. It is a very beautiful, simple title; so simple that it would be easy to overlook it. He is also described as the servant of the Lord and as the prophet of God or God's prophet. It is really in these three titles by which Moses is known that I want to talk to you.

There could be no servant of the Lord unless there was a man of God. It is often forgotten in Christian circles that there is no such thing as true and genuine service unless there is true and genuine humanity. Theological seminaries or Bible schools cannot turn out [produce] servants of God. They can prune away certain things, they can cut out certain things, and they can instruct us in facts, in theology, even in preaching. I do not want to run down any of that, but the idea that the theological seminary can produce a fully fledged servant of God after a couple of years in such a place is a fallacy. And one of the problems in Christian work is that we have had so many people turned out who think they are servants of God but who are not truly servants of the Lord. There can be no servant of the Lord unless first there is a man of God. Let me just say that this is a generic word; it means women of God as well. I know we live in days of feminism and everything else but I hope that it hardly needs to be said here that when we speak of a man of God, it is the woman of God as well.

It is important to underline this very simple fact, that if a person does not become *God's* man, *God's* woman, he cannot become a servant of the Lord. He cannot become the Lord's servant nor can he become a prophet. Whether it is in some other ministry or function that we might have in the body of Christ, the fact still remains that the primary, initial matter is to be God's man or woman. Out of that comes everything else. In other words, if there is no genuine, spiritual character worked into us by the Spirit of God through the work of the Lord Jesus on Calvary, there can never be any acceptable service.

So this matter of spiritual character and service are linked together. Perhaps we see this more clearly in the life of Moses than any other of God's servants and prophets. The lessons that we see in his life are clearly and simply defined. They are drawn in very bold lines so that we can easily understand.

The Calling of God

The first lesson we learn from the life of Moses is all to do with the calling of God. How few believers have any idea as to their calling! This word *calling* is everywhere in the New Testament. We are told to "walk worthily of the calling wherewith we are called" both in Ephesians 4:1 and 1 Thessalonians 2:12. In Philippians 3, in his unbelievable testimony, Paul says, "I press on towards the goal unto the prize of the on-high calling of God in Christ Jesus." Throughout the New Testament you will find this word calling.

Some people think calling is being saved, but actually your salvation is to bring you into the calling of God. The calling of God is more than your salvation. Of course, you cannot know the calling of God unless you are saved. If you are not born of God, if you have not been saved by the grace of God, then you cannot know the calling of God. There is no calling of God on an unsaved life. But once you have been saved by the grace of God, then you have a calling and that calling is a tremendous calling.

Drawn Out

We see this illustrated in Moses' life right from the beginning. His very name in Hebrew, *Mosheh*, means "drawn out." It means someone who was, as it were, delivered and drawn out. Pharaoh's daughter heard the child crying and saw that little ark floating in the water. She called to her ladies-in-waiting to wade out and bring it in, and they found the baby. So she said, "I will call him Mosheh because he was drawn out of the water." And in the Hebrew the past tense is *mashah*. So they called him Mosheh, "drawn out."

Actually, that is exactly what has happened to you and me. We have been drawn out and brought into a whole new world. Little Moses had no idea on that day when he was drawn out of the water that he was being drawn out of Egypt. It looked as if he was being put into the topmost home in Egypt, but actually he was being drawn out of Egypt into another world, into another dimension, into another kingdom, into another people.

If Moses had not been drawn out and delivered, it would have meant certain death in the end. A policeman, a security guard, someone faithful to the Pharaoh and filled with hatred for God's people, would have heard that child's cry and would have destroyed the child. Therefore if Moses had not been drawn out, it would have certainly meant death, and if not death, at the very least, minimally, slavery and bondage for his whole life.

Now think for a moment about yourself. If God had not drawn you out and saved you, it would have been certain death. It would have been a living death, followed by an eternal death. It would have been minimally a life of slavery and bondage without any freedom at all.

Delivered Out of Darkness

I think of that wonderful verse that always means so much to me in Colossians 1:13: "Who delivered us out of the power of darkness, and transferred us into the kingdom of His dear Son." What a marvelous word! Delivered out of the power of darkness; transferred into the kingdom of God's dear Son. Isn't that wonderful! The weakest, simplest, most ignorant child of God has been delivered from the power of darkness and transferred into the kingdom of God's dear Son. We may not know it, but that is the meaning of our salvation. Satan tries to maintain his purchase hold on us. He tries by propaganda to make us believe that he has got a grip on our lives, that he has got an entrenched investment in our lives, but the truth is that we are delivered. If we have been truly born of God, then inherent within our birth is a deliverance from the powers of darkness, a cutting off from the powers of darkness, severance from Satan and that whole hierarchy, and a transferring into the kingdom of God's dear Son. This is true of the weakest, simplest, most ignorant saint.

We do not want you to be weak; we want you to be strong in the Lord. We do not want you to be ignorant; we want you to know the Lord fully. We do not want you to be simple in the sense that you are a bit stupid; we want you to be wise in the Lord. But the fact of the matter is that even if you are weak, young, and stupid, if you are a child of God this is your calling. You have been called *out* of the grip of the power of darkness and transferred into the kingdom of God's dear Son. You are under another sovereignty; you are under another kingship; you are under another power. You are under the Lordship and headship of Jesus. This is your calling. It is marvelous when you think about it.

Called Out of Bondage

You are called out of bondage. Oh, the bondage amongst God's people! Many of the Lord's people have got blinkers [blinders] on. They can only see certain things in the way they have been brought up culturally, the way they have been brought up denominationally, the way of their background. Some people are white; they have white blinkers. People who are black have black blinkers. People who are another color have another color blinkers. We Jews have Jewish blinkers. Gentiles have Gentile blinkers. It is unbelievable. We have these blinkers. Somehow it gives us square vision. We only see certain things. We cannot see the whole counsel of God. We cannot have our horizons broadened. We are in bondage.

Sometimes we are in bondage to impulses, to lusts, to desires, to tendencies of this world. We cannot get free. We know that our sin has been canceled; we know that we have been justified in the sight of God, but the bondage is there. And yet if you are a child of God you have been called out of bondage into God's freedom. Now this freedom does not mean you can just do anything. But it does mean that you are free; you are a truly free person. You are so free you are free to die; you are free to lay down your life. You are free to know an enormous powerful baptism of the Holy Spirit. That is how free you are. Some people are not free. They are bound. Some people are in bondage to the fashions of this world. I know that amongst the Lord's people everything is fashionable that was fashionable forty years ago. It is a very strange thing with the people of God. They only accept as a right what was the fashion fifty or sixty years ago. I do not mean that you should be some fuddy-duddy, dowdy and unattractive.

When we were children, I used to sit behind some sisters, and I really wanted to do something with their hair myself. It was so awful. I used to wonder when one sister last washed her hair. They were supposed to be so spiritual, you see; terribly spiritual people. They were so spiritual they just wanted to walk with God. They were no testimony. When I say bondage to fashion I mean bondage to the concepts of this world. That is a different thing. To be attractive, to be contemporary, not to be a slave to contemporary fashion, especially when it is wrong, but to be a temple of the living God, to be an expression of the Lord is a marvelous thing.

But I am talking about bondage to concepts. You have no idea what humanism is doing in the church. People have their own concepts of this world, and they are even now subjecting the word of God to those concepts and making it say what *they* think it should say in the light of modern fashions. A good example is one of the Methodist groups which has just adopted an alternative Lord's Prayer: "Our mother who art in heaven. Hallowed be thy name." Can you believe that? As if any believer has ever thought that God is only male. God is God. It is unbelievable to me! Because God is in their mind as a projection of the human mind, they have to somehow or other change His whole fashion to make Him more contemporary. Isn't it stupid!

God has called us out of bondage into His marvelous freedom, this glorious freedom. Galatians 5:13 says, "For ye, brethren, were called for freedom; only use not your freedom for an occasion to the flesh, but through love be servants one to another." There is freedom.

Called Out of Darkness

Here is something very wonderful about our calling. We are "... called out of darkness into His marvelous light" (1 Peter 2:9b). When there is darkness in the believer's life, it is a tragedy. It is a contradiction in terms. We are to be light in the Lord. We are "children of light," in another place "sons of light." That shows growth, more responsibility. We are to be light in the Lord. Oh, if we could only understand a little bit about this calling!

Called Out of the World

Then I think of yet another Scripture—Leviticus 25:38. We are called out of this world into Christ. That is the heart of the matter. Called out of this world into Christ.

"Wherefore if any man be in Christ, he is a new creature: the old things are passed away; behold, they are become new" (II Corinthians 5:17). Mr. Austin-Sparks used to say that he did not like this rendering because he felt it made people look at themselves. He liked the other rendering which is just as faithful to the Greek: "Wherefore if any man be in Christ, *there* is a new creation: old things are passed away; behold, all things are become new." Where is the new creation? In Christ. That is where you are part of the new creation—in Christ. We have been called out of the world into Christ, out of the old creation into the new creation, out of the old man into the new man. That is a calling. It is tremendous. That is the very meaning of our salvation.

Called Out of Vanity

We are called out of vanity, out of emptiness, out of hopelessness, aimlessness into God's eternal glory. Vanity! Many Christian lives are filled with vanity. Many Christian lives are filled with emptiness.

When I was young in the Lord I could never understand the little book of Ecclesiastes, that tiny little book in the Old Testament. I used to think to myself: "What is this book doing here?" Then I discovered in my studies that the Rabbis had discussed for years and years whether Ecclesiastes should be in the Scriptures because when you think about it Ecclesiastes is the philosophy of Jean Paul Sartre—existentialism: "Eat, drink, be merry, tomorrow we die." What has it got to do with the word of God?

If it is King Solomon, and I believe it was, he said he built great parks, marvelous buildings, and so on, but he said, "It is vanity, vanity, all is vanity. I have to leave it all." Then he said, "I have seen people who have amassed a great fortune, leave it to their sons, and they squander it within a few months. Emptiness, emptiness, all is emptiness." Then he says, "Marriage—what is that?" He should know because he had a thousand wives. In the end he said, "You live for so long and then you die. Then what?" It is all so negative.

Ecclesiastes has some wonderful little nuggets here and there of marvelous wisdom that you feel you should take out if you were a liberal and attach somewhere else in the Bible and get rid of the rest. But I believe you can never ever read Ecclesiastes without the Song of Solomon. You have these two little books together. One is emptiness, emptiness, all is emptiness; vanity, vanity, all is vanity; aimlessness, aimlessness, all is aimlessness. The other book is purposefulness, purposefulness, all is purposeful; value, value, all is value. The little Song of Solomon transforms the whole picture. Suddenly it is as if, as we believe in Jewish tradition, it was a vision given to Solomon of the love of God for the redeemed, for His own chosen people. It is almost as if God says, "Everything apart from this is vanity, vanity, all is vanity."

But if you have been saved by the grace of God, if you have been called, if you know what your calling is, if you commit yourself to your calling, if you walk worthily of that calling by the grace of God and the power of the Holy Spirit, if you press on toward the goal, then your whole life with all its negative circumstances, unpleasant situations, the times when there seems to be so much that is inexplicable, is all turned to value, value, all is value. It is the calling of the Lord to be the bride of the Lord Jesus, to be the wife of the Lamb, to grow up into Him, to come to full growth, to become a complete person in the Lord Jesus, to grow with others to be His bride. When you understand that, then you understand your calling.

Dear child of God, all this is in Moses' name; an extraordinary man, this Moses. He lived out this calling throughout his life. This calling of God that delivered Moses from certain death and slavery brought him into all the treasures of God. This is the first lesson.

Are you walking worthily of this calling? Just wait; do you know what this calling is? Have you ever bothered to seek the Lord for light? Are you so familiar with Christian things, that you sing the hymns, read the Bible, gather with God's people, and you have never bothered to ask the Lord to instruct you in what your calling really is? How can you walk worthily of a calling you do not understand?

The one thing about Moses is that by the grace of God, or as it says in the New Testament, by the power of the Holy Spirit, he walked worthily of this calling. We have no idea when it first began to dawn on him what it was. We do not know where it came from. Jewish tradition tells us, and that is why we put such a tremendous emphasis on motherhood in Judaism, that it was Moses' mother who was employed. She was actually paid wages to look after her own son. Can you believe that! It is just like the Lord to give the double portion. She got her son, which would have been enough for her even if she had to live like a pauper, but she got wages. And I imagine they were royal wages. So it was really something. And our tradition tells us that she was very careful to teach Moses from his earliest days that he was not really an Egyptian. He had another kind of calling.

The very calling of God was written into his being. He had been drawn out of the river Nile, and God had a purpose for him. We do not know where it first came to him that he was to be a deliverer, but he tried to do it himself. He thought they would all know, but they did not. It was a great shock to him when he found that they rejected him and were ignorant of what God had shown him. But somewhere in his youth, somewhere along the line in his teens, this calling began to dawn upon him even though he was still mixed up with the Egyptian court and everything to do with the Egyptian social life. It was as if slowly, slowly, slowly it dawned on him he was not an Egyptian. He did not belong to Egypt. He had no destiny within Egypt. It was like a spiritual schizophrenic to try and be an Egyptian and at the same time a Jew. There are an awful lot of Christian schizophrenics. They cannot reconcile their life in this world with their calling, and so they try to be good Egyptians.

Total and Costly Commitment

The second lesson is also a very simple one; it is a total and costly commitment to the Lord. You younger people will never regret it to the day you die if you commit yourself totally to the Lord whatever the cost. When I was first saved, I was just thirteen; interestingly, near the age of our Bar Mitzvah. I did not have Bar Mitzvah because I was not brought up in the Jewish tradition. My identity was hidden because of the Nazis. But I found the Lord just before I was thirteen, and it was within months of coming to the Lord that I made a total commitment. Now I was young, and I had no idea of Christian things. I only knew that the Lord Jesus had appeared to me and He had saved me. I remember saying, even though I had no idea what it meant, "Whatever the cost, Lord, I commit myself to You. I want to be wholly for You. I do not want to be a hypocrite. I do not want to join the great number of hypocrites. I want to be for You, wholly with You, a follower of You, a disciple." I do not regret it. It has cost me a tremendous amount, I have to say, just from a human point of view. Of the many things I might have been able to do in this world, they are refuse. Some of you young people may not feel like that just at present. You feel the world is glittering, beautiful, and attractive. And it is calling you to all kinds of things you could be in it and do in it. But this whole world could be turned into a horror by tomorrow morning by just a few catastrophes. And when you have really committed yourself to the Lord, then you know where you are. You never regret it.

Moses—A Prince in Egypt

We see this lesson in Moses. He had so much to lose from one viewpoint if he truly followed the Lord. He was the Pharaoh's daughter's son. This was his title—Son of Pharaoh's Daughter, Grandson of the Pharaoh. This meant he was a royal prince in a hierarchy that was absolute. To belong to the royal family, to be a member of Pharaoh's household, just simply to be one of the officials in the household, one of the viziers, one of the wise men, was a status that people would give anything to have. But to be a prince, to be a grandson of the Pharaoh himself, I say that is something tremendous. That would give you a start in life.

Many people say, "Oh, if I only had a start in life!" In the American dream you do not really understand this thing. All Americans are born equal. The whole thing about American life is success, and anyone can become a success. One of the troubles we have in fellowship is this tremendous success syndrome. It is marvelous in one way and terrible in another. Every male, and now of course we have this new movement with the women as well, everyone has got to be a success. It does not matter how you achieve it as long as you become a success. You may have to damage others, exploit others, manipulate others, but you have got to be a success. So when we come to the Lord's work, we suddenly find everyone eyeing some small fellowship as a prospective platform, a kind of little empire in which we can somehow build up a name for ourselves and so fulfill a ministry. Then come the jealousies, the rivalries, and the bitternesses. It is all part of the success syndrome. Can you imagine what it is like to be born in a kingdom and not a republic? You cannot. You gave it all up two hundred plus years ago, and for this reason you cannot imagine what it is like to be born in a kingdom. But in a kingdom, unless you have blue blood, unless you have the right family, the right background, and the right connections, it is very, very hard to get anywhere, especially in the old days.

But Moses was actually catapulted into the royal family, not simply as a courtier, or as a servant, or as someone who was not of the royal blood, but as someone who was grandson of the Pharaoh himself and had the title of prince. What a start he had! Now Moses knew very well that if he was going to follow the Lord, that is what he was going to have to lose. He was going to have to surrender that. He was going to have to let go of that.

Moses—Mighty In Words

In that passage in Acts 7, Stephen's tremendous message before the Sanhedrin, he says that Moses was mighty in words and works. Then it speaks about the wisdom of Egypt. Now the wisdom of Egypt in antiquity was like today, everything was technological, scientific, factual—all knowledge, all wisdom. It was synonymous with the summit of everything. If you wanted to be anything, go to Egypt. If you wanted to learn anything, go to Egypt. If you wanted to get anywhere, get into the wisdom of Egypt. Moses had a start in all this. He did not have to work his way up. He would have found it very hard as a foreigner, even as an Egyptian. He was in the royal family.

If you understand that, then you understand amazing things about Moses. You understand that he was right in this world of learning, in this world of academic understanding and knowledge. Do not think of Moses as he is portrayed in some Christian things of doubtful origin as some smelly Bedouin shepherd who was wandering around illiterate. They used to say Moses could not read or write, so he could not have possibly ever been the editor of Genesis. Now, of course, they have discovered in the last hundred years or more that the Egyptians in fact had an alphabet. They never understood all those funny little hieroglyphs, and they just thought they were pictures. Being good Westerners with an alphabet, they had no idea that it was a language. Now we know that the Egyptians had a language. And furthermore, someone brought up as Pharaoh's daughter's son would have been unbelievably educated and instructed in the wisdom of the Egyptians. The concepts and the fashions of Egypt were the things that Moses was brought up in. It was his culture, his background. Remember that.

Moses—Mighty in Works

Then there is another thing. It says he was mighty in works. We often wonder in what way he was mighty when, for instance, whoever wrote the letter to the Hebrews says that he chose the reproach of Christ and ill treatment with the people of God rather than the treasures of Egypt and the pleasures of sin for a season. It is just a little intimation of something. But in our tradition we understand that Moses was one of the great military generals and heroes of his day in the Libyan and Ethiopian campaigns of that Pharaoh. He was idolized as a popular folk hero throughout Egypt. That meant every door was open to Moses.

Now if you take all this, you begin to understand that when Moses chose the reproach of Christ as it says, it really was the reproach of Christ. People could not understand what this prince was doing. This great hero, this learned young man turned his back on the whole of this and went out into the desert. What was wrong with the man? Even later when he came back and said things like, "The Lord says, 'Israel is My firstborn son. Let My firstborn son go and serve Me,'" the Egyptians could not understand it. What in the world is the man talking about? Does he really mean this bunch of slaves, these poor people? Does he really think that they are something to throw one's lot in with rather than Egypt? Egypt—the great, Egypt—Egypt of the pyramids, Egypt of the Nile, Egypt of great cities, Egypt of the Sphinx. And is he going to wander out in the desert with this rag-tag bunch of Hebrew slaves? He is crazy. He will go down in history as a nut case.

But Moses has not gone down in history as a nut case. Even the world at large recognizes Moses as one of the greatest personalities and characters in world history with probably the greatest influence ever wielded through history and succeeding generations of any man of his day. It has been proven beyond all doubt that by a total and costly commitment to the Lord, Moses' name is eternal. His name is associated with our Lord Jesus, associated with the throne of God, associated with the kingdom of God, associated with the purpose of God. Even when nations are no more, the name of Moses will be known. It was a total and costly commitment.

Moses Gave up the Treasures of Egypt

What does it mean "the pleasures of Egypt"? What does it mean "pleasures of sin for a season"? Most of us who are a little older know that sin can be very pleasurable for a very short time, then you pay the price for it. Why did Moses choose the reproach of Christ rather than the treasures of Egypt? Why did he choose to suffer ill-treatment with the people of God rather than to know the pleasures of sin for a season? I will tell you. You can only choose such a calling if you have seen the Lord and you have living faith. Nobody else can do it. You can sing about it; you can study it; you can even pray about it, but nobody will ever totally commit himself or herself to the Lord in a costly way unless it is by living faith. Living faith is the heart of this matter. It is by faith that Moses forsook Egypt, and it is by faith that you and I ever totally commit ourselves to the Lord and to what is called the reproach of Christ.

A Living Sacrifice

I think of the apostle Paul's amazing cry as it is recorded in Romans 12:1: "I beseech you therefore, brethren, by the mercies of God, that you present your bodies a living sacrifice, holy, acceptable to God, which is your spiritually, intelligent worship. And be not conformed to this world or to the fashions of this world, but be ye transformed by the renewing of your mind, that you may prove what is the good and perfect and acceptable will of God."

What was the apostle Paul referring to? He was referring to that whole eight chapters in which he had expounded the gospel, the good news, and he said if you understand this gospel, don't dilly-dally, don't dither, don't hesitate. Totally commit yourself. If you are young, give your whole life to the Lord from the beginning. You will never regret it. Perhaps you are older and have wasted your middle-age in that marvelous period where everything is sort of spreading out, that time when somehow or other you have lost the first zeal, even for sin. You have lost all those marvelous dynamic feelings you once had when you were younger. You do not want to admit it. You try, especially in North America, to keep young, but it is gone. It is not too late to totally commit yourself to the Lord. And if, per chance, there should be those who are old and have never totally committed their lives to the Lord (what a tragedy to have lived a life in an Egyptian context), it is not too late. Better late than never.

The apostle Paul says in the light of this amazing good news of the grace of God in the Lord Jesus, "Present your bodies a living sacrifice. This is your spiritually intelligent worship." Many of us know something about emotional worship, and I am not despising it. It is wonderful when we are carried along and inspired in a moment of worship. Suddenly we are in the presence of God. But spiritually intelligent worship is cold blooded. It means you have laid down your life, and that in the eyes of God is real worship. Now your whole being—spirit, soul, and body—has been offered as a living sacrifice to God, holy, acceptable to Him. This is your spiritually intelligent worship. And it is this spiritually intelligent worship that leads you not to be conformed to this world, to the ideas and concepts of this world, but to be transformed by the renewing of your mind, and so to prove what is the good and perfect and acceptable will of God. This is your calling. You can have your calling; you can even understand your calling, but if you do not totally commit yourself to the Lord at whatever the cost in your life, it will never be realized fully.

It is amazing to me that Romans 9, 10, and 11 are all to do with election, and I believe that is just as important as the gospel. You have to have these two things together, and now suddenly you understand that in the light of this election Paul says, "Present your bodies a living sacrifice." Do you realize you are chosen?

Do you realize you are elect? Do you realize what God has in mind for you? Do you realize all the wonders that God has compressed into this salvation of ours in Christ? You will only begin to know it when you present your bodies a living sacrifice.

This total commitment led directly to Moses' training, education, and discipline. If I may put it another way, and this may sound very offensive to you to begin with, God never casts pearls before swine because they turn and tread them under foot as if they were rubbish. What does this mean? It means that God will not open His heart to you—He will save you, but He will not open His heart to you, He will not reveal His secrets to you, He will not begin your discipline, He will not start your education or training until you commit yourself to Him. If you think that as a careless child of God, treating in a familiar way the things of God, you are going to be educated by God, you have another think coming. You could be a whole generation that wanders around the wilderness for forty years and gets nowhere. You can see the acts of God, the great signs of God, the wonders of God, the provision of God, the direction of God, the word of God, even the tabernacle of God, and not be in it. You go round and round and round and round again. Only when you commit yourself to the Lord does the Holy Spirit begin your education. But when you have committed yourself to the Lord, your education begins. The school of God starts. Your training camp starts. The discipline begins. It is an amazing thing with the Lord, but He does not discipline those who are not going to go on to sonship. If you want to be treated as a babe and a child He will go on doing that. You can opt out if you will, but once you have committed yourself to the Lord your education begins. This I believe is a very big lesson.

Moses' Big Problem—Himself

Let me go back to Moses. Moses was called. Moses had now begun to understand his calling and had committed himself to the Lord even though it cost him everything. But Moses had an enormous problem. His problem was neither Pharaoh nor Pharaoh's daughter; his problem was himself. Many, many Christians who have begun to understand the calling of God, who have responded to the Lord and committed themselves to the Lord, do not know how to handle their self-life. They suddenly discover they have within them a self-life that is as ambitious as it was in Egypt, as unbroken as it was in Egypt, as desirous for power as it was in Egypt, as determined to get to the top as it was in Egypt. This is the problem.

The Principle of Preparation

Alone for Forty Years

And that leads me to the last lesson I want to underline. It is the principle of preparation. Forty years Moses was prepared. Forty years of preparation! Did he have a leadership course? What kind of preparation did he have? Maybe he went through whole courses that were very practical. No. The extraordinary thing with Moses was that there was hardly another person in sight. He had Jethro, his father-in-law, and Zipporah his dear wife, who according to our tradition was somewhat difficult, and his two sons. This is an extraordinary way for a man to be trained to lead a nation, to be the founder of a nation. You mean he gave up everything in Egypt and was alone for forty years? Basically, yes.

A Keeper of Sheep

Another extraordinary thing is that he kept sheep and goats and camels. Now I would think this is hardly a normally recognized way of being trained for service. Sheep are stupid creatures, although I think they are very loving. In our part of the world people sometime keep them for pets like dogs. You see them on a leash going through the souk to their owner's stall. It is not a big surprise when you see a great big cuddly creature, like an English sheep dog, sitting there with a docile look on its face, with a bell under its neck, munching, forever chewing the cud round and round and round. Goats are far more intelligent and infinitely more smelly. And camels are extraordinary creatures. Someone once said a camel was the creation of a committee trying to make a horse. I think this is a very unkind way of looking at the camel. The camel is one of the most extraordinary creatures. Every time I look at a camel I think that only God could have created him. Nobody else in the world would have ever thought of such a creature.

They say that the camel has that haughty look because men know one hundred names for God but the camel knows one hundred and one names, and that is why he looks so haughty at you. And the camel is another very smelly creature.

Poor Moses, brought up in all the perfumed beauty of the palaces of Egypt, bathed in asses' milk, powdered and pampered with a thousand servants, and there he was alone in the desert with smelly sheep and goats and camels. Now I could have understood it if the Lord had given him one year there. That is how most of us would have understood it. We would have said that would do anybody good. It would humble them, bring them face to face with reality, get them out of that pulpit mentality, help them to face themselves. Maybe five years would be good for some, and some with unbelievably strong personalities, maybe ten. But forty years! Forty years in the Jewish tradition is a generation, a whole lifetime.

Waiting

Dear child of God, it is exactly the same with us in principle. This preparation of God for eternal service is a lifetime matter. Your kitchen sink, your children, your difficult relative, your business life, your work-a-day life, and our fellowship are the sphere of such preparation. If I were asked to put in a word what the heart of this preparation is I would say straightaway: it is waiting. Now this is the one thing that the flesh cannot do. It cannot wait. Moses knew he was going to be deliverer of the people of God. But year after year goes by, and he waits and waits and waits and waits, just like Abraham had waited for that son that never came for so long. Waiting is the best way to bring an uncrucified self-life to its end. And most of us cannot wait. We cannot even wait with one another. If we see someone who is not baptized, we wait for a week while we pray that the Lord will speak to him or her. Then we wait for two weeks, or maybe a month, and when we see that the Holy Spirit is not speaking to them, we fulfill the need. We jump in and do it all. We are all the same with one another in this way. We wait for the Lord to do it and if He does not do it, don't worry, we will step in. We will do that work for the Lord. Waiting!

Isn't it interesting that in the book of James it says, "Let patience have her perfect work, that ye may be perfect and entire, lacking in nothing." Patience, endurance is the word, steadfastness is the crown of all God's work in our lives. What is he saying? He says, "And let patience, [endurance] have its perfect work, that ye may be perfect, complete, and entire, lacking in nothing." Endurance infers waiting. This kind of preparation is a principle with God.

Abraham—you see a whole lifetime of preparation. At the end of it was nothing but a few square meters to be buried in. Jacob—a lifetime of manipulation in the energy of his life until finally he comes to Jabbok and he is changed into Israel. Joseph—years and years in a dungeon until God lifts him up and makes him ruler of Egypt. David—nearly twenty years of wandering with Saul after him in preparation to be king. I could speak of John the Baptist, even of Paul, who was three years in the Syrian Desert being prepared.

Moses' Rod

God put it all in a nutshell in a very extraordinary picture. When finally the Lord appeared to Moses in the desert at the end of this forty years of preparation, Moses was different. He said, "I cannot do it." Before, he would have been straightaway in the forefront of the whole thing. Now he says, "I cannot do it." And the Lord said, "What is that in your hand?" Moses said, "My rod." Now this rod was the thing he used to prod the sheep. He was never without it—a staff and a rod. This rod was going to be the symbol of all Moses' authority in the days to come. Many miracles would be wrought in the sight of God's people and in the sight of the Egyptians by this rod. Now the Lord said, "What is that in your hand?" "It is my rod." And the Lord said to him, "Cast it down." He cast it down and instantly it became a snake. But it was not just a snake; it was a sand viper, one of the most poisonous of all our snakes in Israel. Moses had lived forty years in the desert and knew all about sand vipers. Then the Lord said to him, "Take it up by the tail." Most of you will know that the one thing you do not do with a sand viper is take it up by its tail. There may be others that you take up by the tail, but certainly not a sand viper. You are a dead person if you take up such a snake by the tail. Moses took it up by the tail and it became a rod. Don't you think it was the biggest shock that Moses ever had when he realized that that rod he used to sleep with beside his pillow had a sand viper in it? that that rod he used again and again to prod the sheep with and which seemed to be for him such a comforting thing actually had a sand viper in it? He had no idea that there was a sand viper, a poisonous snake in that rod.

The Self-Life

This is a picture of you and me. Our self-life is just like that. We have no idea that within it is the poison of hell. It is only when we have let go of our self-life and laid it down that its real nature comes out into the open, and for the first time we understand that the very poison of hell is within our self-life. Now there are some people who are naturally very sweet and sentimental, so you think they are not like that. Do not kid yourself. That self-life has poison in it, and I have found that the sweetest, most sentimental people, once they get aggravated and angry, become the most vicious, and sometimes the most cruel. Something comes out of them that you would never have thought was there. But it is there given the right circumstances.

Most of us when we really see ourselves cannot forgive ourselves. We are so proud. When we really see what is in us, we think the Lord is shocked. If the Lord had known this He would never have saved me. My dear friends, the Lord knew that when He saved you. Before you were born He knew the whole thing. He is not shocked; you are shocked. You have discovered there is a snake inside your self-life. That is the principle of preparation. The waiting is to bring you to the place where you understand that something in there can destroy you and destroy others unless you lay it down. Why do you think the Lord said to His disciples, "If any man come after Me, let him deny himself, take up his cross and follow Me; he that seeks to preserve his life, the same shall lose it; he that loses his life for My sake and for the gospel, shall find it"?

Do you remember how this all began? It began with Peter trying to stop the Lord from going to the cross. And the Lord turned around and said, "Get behind Me, Satan." It was a terrible shock to Peter to be called Satan. The Lord did not say, "You are thinking negative thoughts." That would have been very pleasant. Or He could have said, "Peter, Satan is tampering with your mind." That would have been okay. No. He said, "Get behind Me, Satan." It was the snake in Peter's self-life. Then the Lord Jesus went on and said, "If any man come after Me, let him deny himself, [give up all rights to himself,] take up his cross and follow Me." In other words, you will only ever find out what is in you when you give yourself up.

Then the Lord said something else to Moses. He said, "Put your hand in your bosom." He put it in his bosom next to his heart. "Now take it out." He took it out and it was white with leprosy.

In other words, it was not just the start of leprosy; it had gone right into nearly the final stages. Then the Lord said, "Put that hand back in." He put it in and took it out and it was clean. Isn't that interesting! What holds the rod? The hand. What do we do with our hands? We work with them. Here we are back to character.

Then the Lord said to Moses, "If they do not believe this, there is one last thing. Take water from the river and pour it out on the dry ground." It became blood. I often wondered about this. It is clear that these were some of the signs that Moses did in Egypt in Pharaoh's presence but why did the Lord have this tremendous lesson about the rod, the hands, and now the water? Then I thought of I John 5: "Whatsoever is born of God overcomes the world, and who is this that overcomes the world but he that believes that Jesus is the Son of God? Jesus Christ came not by water only but by the water and by the blood. And there are three that bear witness—the Spirit, the water, and the blood." In other words, water speaks of life and blood speaks of grace. I believe what the Lord was saying to Moses was this: "You have to understand that your whole life has to be lived on the basis of My grace—blood and water—then you will overcome. This is the Son of God. This is preparation. This is a principle. May the Holy Spirit make it a living reality to every one of us.

Shall we pray:

Lord, we want to ask together that you take these lessons from the life of Moses, the man of God, and write them on our hearts. Reveal these things to us, Lord. There are things we have not understood fully, other things we have understood. Make those things our experience, Lord. And what we do not understand, reveal to us and make it our experience in days to come. And we shall give You all the praise and the glory. We ask this in the name of our Lord Jesus. Amen.

2.
The Servant of the Lord

Exodus 3:1–6, 13–15

Now Moses was keeping the flock of Jethro his father-in-law, the priest of Midian: and he led the flock to the back of the wilderness, and came to the mountain of God, unto Horeb. And the angel of the Lord appeared unto him in a flame of fire out of the midst of a bush: and he looked, and, behold, the bush burned with fire, and the bush was not consumed. And Moses said, I will turn aside now, and see this great sight, why the bush is not burnt. And when the Lord saw that he turned aside to see, God called unto him out of the midst of the bush, and said, Moses, Moses. And he said, Here am I. And he said, Draw not nigh hither: put off thy shoes from off thy feet, for the place whereon thou standest is holy ground. Moreover he said, I am the God of thy father, the God of Abraham, the God of Isaac, and the God of Jacob. And Moses hid his face; for he was afraid to look upon God.

And Moses said unto God,

Behold, when I come unto the children of Israel, and shall say unto them, The God of your fathers hath sent me unto you; and they shall say to me, What is his name? What shall I say unto them? And God said unto Moses, I AM THAT I AM: and he said, Thus shalt thou say unto the children of Israel, I AM hath sent me unto you. And God said moreover unto Moses, Thus shalt thou say unto the children of Israel, the Lord, the God of your fathers, the God of Abraham, the God of Isaac, and the God of Jacob, hath sent me unto you: this is my name for ever, and this is my memorial unto all generations.

Exodus 4:1

And Moses answered and said, But, behold, they will not believe me, nor hearken unto my voice; for they will say, the Lord hath not appeared unto thee. And the Lord said unto him, What is that in thy hand? And he said, A rod. And he said, Cast it on the ground. And he cast it on the ground, and it became a serpent; and Moses fled from before it. And the Lord said unto Moses, Put forth thy hand, and take it by the tail (and he put forth his hand, and laid hold of it, and it became a rod in his hand); that they may believe that the Lord, the God of their fathers, the God of Abraham, the God of Isaac, and the God of Jacob, hath appeared unto thee. And the Lord said furthermore unto him, Put now thy hand into thy bosom. And he put his hand into his bosom: and when he took it out, behold, his hand was leprous, as white as snow. And he said, Put thy hand into thy bosom again. (And he put his hand into his bosom again; and when he took it out of his bosom, behold, it was turned

again as his other flesh.) And it
shall come to pass, if they will
not believe thee, neither hearken
to the voice of the first sign, that
they will believe the voice of the
latter sign. And it shall come
to pass, if they will not believe
even these two signs, neither
hearken unto thy voice, that
thou shalt take of the water of
the river, and pour it upon the
dry land: and the water which
thou takest out of the river shall
become blood upon the dry land.

II Corinthians 4:7–12, 16–18
But we have this treasure
in earthen vessels, that the
exeeding greatness of the power
may be of God, and not from
ourselves; we are pressed on
every side, yet not straitened;
perplexed, yet not unto despair;
pursued, yet not forsaken;
smitten down, yet not destroyed;

always bearing about in the
body the dying of Jesus, that
the life also of Jesus may be
manifested in our body. For we
who live are always delivered
unto death for Jesus' sake, that
the life also of Jesus may be
manifested in our mortal flesh.
So then death worketh in us, but
life in you.

Wherefore we faint not; but
though our outward man is
decaying, yet our inward man
is renewed day by day. For
our light affliction, which is
for the moment, worketh for us
more and more exceedingly an
eternal weight of glory; while we
look not at the things which are
seen, but at the things which are
not seen: for the things which
are seen are temporal; but the
things which are not seen are
eternal.

In the first letter of the apostle Paul to the church at Corinth he writes, "Now these things happened unto them by way of example; and they were written for our admonition, upon whom the ends of the ages are come" (1 Corinthians 10:11). So I am taking some of the lessons from the life of Moses. We have already underlined three lessons—the calling of God, total and costly commitment to the Lord, and the principle of preparation.

Now I want to take a further three lessons. This matter of spiritual character and service that we are seeking to underline and illustrate from the life of Moses is all important. It is a sobering fact for believers to remember that when they come to die, as all of us will without exception if the Lord does not return, the only thing we carry into eternity is what the Lord has done in us. It does not matter if we have built a great business empire, or obtained enormous property, or have many degrees after our name; it does not matter the kind of work we have done amongst the Lord's people in one sense, we have to leave everything. As the Scripture puts it, "Naked we came into this world and naked we go out of it." And the only thing that we take into eternity is what the Lord has done in us. Sometimes it takes Christians a whole lifetime before they begin to understand this simple fact. We fritter away our lives, we argue with the Lord, we allow issues to develop in our lives and families, in our ministries, in our fellowship which should be settled but we will not settle them. So we go through the whole of life frustrating what the Lord is seeking to do in us.

Spiritual character is beyond price. The little book of Ecclesiastes puts it very simply: "Whatsoever the Lord doeth, it is forever. Nothing can be added to it and nothing can be taken away." It is a marvelous thing when God, through our circumstances and situations, does something in our lives that is forever. And service is actually related to spiritual character. If you have little spiritual character, your service will be superficial. If there is not great depth in you, then your service will likewise have little depth in it. Our service is related to our character. So in many ways this matter that we are talking about is of tremendous importance.

The Key to all Fulfillment

I believe this lesson on the key to all fulfillment is the most important lesson in Moses' life. After forty years in the desert, forty years of waiting, forty years of preparation, finally, and only then, does the Lord appear to Moses. Some people just cannot take this in—forty years, four decades, nearly a lifetime, a whole generation, a Biblical generation. Moses was called by God, he committed himself to the Lord, and for forty years he was with smelly sheep, goats, and camels, wandering in a desert with just a few people, mostly relatives. Only at the end of that forty years does the Lord meet with him. This meeting between God and Moses can never be over emphasized. It can never be over valued. Someone may say to me, "I think you are exaggerating this incident a little in its importance." No! This was the point at which the Lord revealed His name, and that has to change our whole attitude to this incident. It was not merely that the Lord met with Moses just in some small and almost trivial way. This was a meeting between God and Moses that has tremendous significance and meaning for the whole redeemed family of God, because the Lord revealed His personal name.

What happened? Moses had been forty years in the desert, keeping goats and sheep, forty years of three hundred and sixty five days apiece, day in and day out, day in and day out. Sheep have to be looked after. Goats are not only more intelligent, they are more disease free. It is a very strange thing, but sheep have to be inspected every day. They are so prone to disease. They are not only silly; they are also prone to disease. And poor Moses had to go day in and day out inspecting the sheep. Some people get very sentimental. They think the shepherd has a great love for all his sheep. Otherwise, why does he know them by name? It is because he has to inspect them every day, so he has names for some of them.

The Burning Bush

After forty years the thing had become, one could say without exaggeration, somewhat routine for Moses. And now on this quite ordinary day with the routine responsibilities and duties of leading the sheep and goats in the desert, Moses noticed a fire. This is not so extraordinary. Very often in the desert a bush ignites spontaneously. I have seen it a number of times myself. The first time I ever saw it I asked the Bedouin who was with me what the fire was, and he looked at me as if I was crazy. He said, "It is a thorn bush gone up in smoke." And so it was. It went up in fire and there was a little puff of smoke, and within a few minutes it was over.

God Speaks From the Bush

Moses saw this fire, turned and looked at it and thought to himself: "It is one of the thorn bushes gone up in smoke." He went on keeping the sheep. He looked again, maybe ten minutes later, and he was a little surprised because it was still burning. So he must have thought to himself: "Some bush." Then he went on dreaming his dreams. He looked back again, perhaps after a half hour, and the bush was still burning. He thought: "Well, that is quite a bush. Maybe it was not so dry; maybe there was still a little sap in it." After another fifteen or twenty minutes, he looked again and thought to himself: "I think I am going to walk over and have a look at that bush because it is still burning with fire, but it is not consumed." When he went across to this very ordinary bush, not higher probably than my waist and that is saying something because most of them are only up to my knees, he saw that the bush burned with fire and the bush was not consumed. Then suddenly he heard the voice of God, not from above, not from behind, but from the bush. It was as if the Lord had gotten into this small bush and was speaking up, as it were, to Moses: "Moses, Moses."

And Moses said, "I am here."

And the Lord said, "Take your shoes from off your feet; the ground whereon you stand is holy." And Moses did precisely that.

Then the Lord said, "I am the God of your father, the God of Abraham, of Isaac, and of Jacob."

What kind of Bush?

Why did the Lord choose this extraordinary way of meeting with one of His own children that was going to become one of the most powerful and influential servants in His whole family? I have often thought to myself, having a vivid imagination, why did the Lord choose one of these bushes? There is great discussion about what this bush is. In the Hebrew it is not just a bush; it is a thorn bush. We know it is a generic thorn bush, but beyond that we do not know what kind of thorn bush it is. In our desert there are a number of thorn bushes. There is the small acacia that would be the biggest of all of the acacia bushes. The camels like it and chew on it. I have often watched them chewing on those great big thorns and wonder how in the world those soft rubbery-like mouths manage to chew on thorns. It could have been that. The general idea among Christians is that it is a blackberry bush. We call it the bramble, and they are found in the Sinai, so it is entirely possible it was a bramble. But our own Israeli scholars believe that it was the ordinary thorn bush. It is the most common bush in the desert. You will see it everywhere. These bushes are tiny, only knee high. They live quickly and die very rapidly. Sometimes you see them blowing around the desert in the wind. The Bedouin do not even like them for fuel because they burn so quickly. And even the camels turn up their noses at them. If they can find anything else to eat they will, rather than eat this humble little bush. God chose the most common thorn bush in the desert in which to meet with Moses. Don't you think that is amazing?

I sometimes think to myself: Why didn't the Lord take a palm tree? Wouldn't that have been magnificent! Think of the Bible commentators and the expositors. I can just imagine it—a great palm with all those fronds and fire bursting out of it. What a fireworks display! Then the Lord would say, "Moses, Moses."

"Here I am, Lord."

He would say, "Take the shoes from off your feet, the ground whereon you stand is holy." The Bible commentators and Bible expositors would have had a field day. They would say, "The palm tree is a picture of righteousness and holiness. Holy, Holy, Holy, is the Lord. The Lord got into the palm tree because He said, 'Take the shoes from off your feet; the ground whereon you stand is holy.'" It would have been marvelous, but the Lord did not choose the palm tree. The Lord has chosen the palm tree as a symbol of holiness and righteousness, but He did not take it.

Or He could have taken the fig tree. That would have been marvelous, especially for us who believe in the future of the Jewish people. We would have said, "Learn the parable of the fig tree." And there in that beautiful tree, with all its lovely green branches, there would have been a blaze of glory. And we would have all said, "Yes, the fig tree is a symbol of the nation." We would have had a ball with this. But the Lord did not choose the fig tree. And there are fig trees in the oasis of the Sinai Desert.

Supposing the Lord had taken a pomegranate. Pomegranates are everywhere; they are native to our part of the world. The pomegranate is so beautiful. That was the shape that was used for the golden bells on the high priests. The pomegranates are a marvelous picture and symbol of fertility. We would have had a marvelous time. "Moses, the people of God have got to multiply, multiply, multiply." Wouldn't we have had a wonderful time with this? But the Lord did not choose the pomegranate.

The Lord could have chosen the vine. Now the vine is not so big, especially our native vines, but they would have made a great big heap. What a wonderful picture! Bible expositors and commentators would have said, "Jesus said, 'I am the true vine.'" We would have said, "The Lord appeared to Moses nearly two thousand years before Jesus said, "I am the true vine"; and He appeared to him out of the midst of the vine. But He did not.

Or, if you are charismatic, think of an olive tree. There are olive trees in the oasis in the Sinai Desert. Can you imagine if the fire had burst out of an olive tree? Everyone would have said, "That's it! It is the Person and work of the Holy Spirit. We have to be filled with the Holy Spirit. And wasn't it fire? Fire in the tree. We need the baptism of the Spirit and of fire." We would have had a wonderful time with it, but the Lord did not choose an olive tree.

There is one other tree you find in the desert and it is everywhere. In the time of Moses, there were many, many more thousands of these trees. In the old King James Version it is the shittim tree, and this is the acacia tree. Now here we really would have had a field day. Can you have imagined it? We could have then tied this in with the tabernacle. We would have said that the wood in the tabernacle was all shittim wood, and when the Lord appeared to Moses, He chose this marvelous acacia tree, a very beautiful tree in its own way. And in a blaze of fire the Lord said, "Moses, Moses." And Moses said, "I am here, Lord." And He would have said, "Take the shoes from off your feet; the ground whereon you stand is holy." We would have said that God is talking about His dwelling place. But the Lord did not choose the acacia tree.

Insignificant Thorn Bush

He chose the most common thorn bush of the desert, two-a-penny, so insignificant you certainly would not plant it in your garden. I know some people who have these wonderful cactus gardens. There are some cactuses that are wonderful. I once had a cactus and it took fourteen years before it flowered. Then after fourteen years it flowered and flowered and flowered, and a thief came over the garden wall and stole it. But nobody would ever plant a thorn bush, not this thorn bush I am talking about. There is nothing about it that is beautiful, honestly. It is the most uninteresting thing.

This was not just a nice green thorn bush flowering with a very uninteresting and insignificant little flower. This was a dead thorn bush. This was a thorn bush that had lived its life, exhausted its energies in its natural life, and died. And now God, may I put it reverently, got into the old insignificant, dead thorn bush.

Moses Was the Thorn Bush

God chose that thorn bush with tremendous significance. That thorn bush was Moses. He thought he was a palm tree; God knew he was a thorn bush. He thought he was an olive tree; God knew he was a thorn bush. He thought he was a pomegranate; God knew he was a thorn bush. He thought he was the acacia tree; God knew he was a thorn bush. He thought he was the vine; God knew he was a thorn bush. Before ever he could become all of those symbolized he had to recognize one simple, essential, basic fact. He was a worthless, dead thorn bush. It had taken the Lord forty years to reduce Moses to that status. At the beginning of those forty years, Moses would never in his wildest imagination have described himself as a thorn bush, certainly not a dead thorn bush, an exhausted thorn bush. But at the end of forty years of waiting, of discipline, of training, of breaking, Moses knew he was a thorn bush. Moses was the thorn bush; God was the flame of fire. And when the flame of fire gets into the dead thorn bush, the bush burns with fire and is not consumed. Then it is holy ground.

You may not know that you are a thorn bush. It takes most of us quite a lifetime before we get to the place where we finally recognize what we really are. But the fact of the matter is this: Christ in you has sanctified you. You are holy ground. It is not the actual thorn bush; it is the fire.

Israel Was the Thorn Bush

Let me take you a step further. It is not just that Moses was the thorn bush; Israel was the thorn bush. It was as if God was saying to Moses, "Moses, you are nothing but a dead thorn bush. I am the fire. But you and I in union will change the world. You and I together will fulfill My purpose. Moses, it is not that you are just the thorn bush. This people that you are going to lead out of Egypt are a thorn bush. You are going to find that out. You are going to find that every time you touch them you touch thorns. They are a worthless, dead thorn bush, but I am in them. If you only see the thorns and come into confrontation with the thorns, you will forget I am in this thorn bush. They are holy ground because I dwell in their midst."

It is as if God was saying to Moses, "When Israel as a dead thorn bush, and I as the living God come together, the bush burns with fire but the bush will never be consumed and history will be made."

The Lesson of Nothingness

This lesson is so tremendous. I just wish that I had the mouth of an angel to communicate to you this tremendous lesson. It is the hardest lesson that the child of God learns—you and I are nothing. After forty years of God dealing with us, we know that we are nothing. Then comes the problem because now we know we are nothing. We know we are incompetent, unable, incapable, insignificant, worthless, and we forget that the key is the flame of fire. For when the flame of fire gets into that old dried up, dead thorn bush, things happen. History is made in your circumstances. God's purpose for you and your family is fulfilled. When you get a company of folks together who know that they are nothing and the Lord is in the midst, then history is made, as far as God is concerned, in that company of His children. You and I could be tempted to write off the thorn bush.

Don't you think that is our problem most of the time? We get into the fellowship of God's people and after awhile we begin to find there are an awful lot of thorns. Then we find there is an awful lot of deadness and an awful lot of worthlessness. Then we begin to come to a wrong conclusion. We think there is nothing here. In fact God is there.

The Church is a Thorn Bush

You see this when the apostle Paul came to the Corinthian church. What a mess it was! Thorns, thorns—they were divided into factions, divisions, human personalities, great teachers and apostles that ranged up behind each of them. They had lawsuits, believer with believer. Some young man was sleeping with his mother. Can you believe it in a church! There was disorder. There was drunkenness at the Lord's Table. (How they ever did that on grape juice I will never know. It was another one of the miracles of the New Testament.) But they got drunk at the Lord's Table. Under the table they went. Now we are not talking about something denominational, something that is traditional, we are talking about the living company of God's children, born of His Spirit. Here was a church most of us would have said, "I'm out of this thing. I will not have anything more to do with it. It is a hellhole. It is just a focal point of everything that is dark and evil and contrary to the will of God." You would have made a tremendous mistake.

The apostle said this in 1 Corinthians 1:7–9: "So that ye come behind in no gift; waiting for the revelation of our Lord Jesus Christ; who shall also confirm you unto the end, that ye be unreprovable in the day of our Lord Jesus Christ. God is faithful, through whom ye were called into the fellowship of his Son Jesus Christ our Lord."

Here is a thorn bush. If you think that the church ought to be something glorious and wonderful, so do I. But if from that you deduce that you are looking for something perfect, you will never find it. The church down here on earth is not meant to be perfect. It is going *on* to perfection, and every time someone is born again, every time there is a new influx of newborn, spiritual babes, you have all the imperfections in the world. There are those who are alcoholics, or drug cases, or perverts, or prostitutes, or pimps, or divorcees, or a thousand and one other things. Think for a moment. Everyone is looking for the perfect church. They are crazy. It was Moody who said, "You are looking for the perfect church? When you join it, it will be imperfect." Of course, we are looking for the Lord to be doing something, but the church down here is a builder's yard. It is a cutting out room. It is a pressure cooker. It is where the work is being done. If anyone tells me they have found the perfect church, I know they have not found a true church. They have found an elitist group. They have not found the church.

The whole point that the Lord was saying to Moses was this: "Moses, first and foremost I want you to know that you are a thorn bush. I am in you. You are the thorn bush. You are dead, and in one sense you remain dead. You remain worthless. You remain a thorn bush all the way through. I will be the fire and you will be eternal fuel for eternal fire."

Moses Forgot He Was a Thorn Bush

Then again you can look at it another way. "Moses, you and Aaron are going to lead this people, but remember, it is a thorn bush. I am in the thorn bush." Maybe you have questioned God's goodness and love when Moses lost his temper with the children of Israel and was told to speak to the rock and he struck it twice and said, "You rebels." And you thought, "Poor Moses." Maybe if you are not in leadership, you do not feel quite the same sympathy for Moses, but I tell you after years in the Lord's work I have tremendous sympathy for Moses. There are times when I feel like whacking God's people. They are so stupid, so critical. Have you ever wondered why God took it out on poor Moses? You think: This man was so faithful. He followed the Lord so fully. He was totally committed to the Lord. And then for one single incident the Lord said, "You are not going over into the land." It was the thorn bush. Moses forgot the lesson of the thorn bush.

The Unmentionable Name of God

When God told Moses He was sending him to the children of Israel, Moses said, "Lord, it is very well for You to tell me to go to our people, but whom do I say sent me?" And then the Lord said, "I AM THAT I AM. Tell them I AM has sent you."

I have heard marvelous messages on this. There have been theological treatises: "God is omnipotent, God is omniscient, no beginning, no end, Creator of heaven and earth, absolutely magnificent, marvelous." I could tell you even the names of some of the brothers that have given these messages over the years about I AM THAT I AM. But it always left me cold. Somehow I could never relate to it, even though I was in awe of the Lord.

Then a little Irishman came to Halford House. He led my stepfather to the Lord. He was as wide, as he was tall. He was so plump he used to put his Bible on his stomach and use it as a pulpit. His name was Johnny Cochran, may the Lord bless him. He had no education; he could not read or write. He came to the Lord through W. P. Nicholson that great Irish evangelist. Because he wanted to learn to know God, he taught himself to read and write by reading the Bible.

He stood up at the end of the Lord's Table one morning and he said, "I believe God has given me this message from Exodus 3. I am going to speak to you this morning about the unmentionable name of God: I AM THAT I AM." I thought to myself: "Johnny you have bitten off a bit too much." Then he said, "I have listened to tremendous messages on this name of the Lord and they have all left me cold." I thought: "I understand that; same here." Then he said, "I went to the Lord and I said, 'Lord, I do not understand your name.'" And the Lord said to me, "My name is a blank check. I AM—fill in whatever you need. Do you need life? I am your life. Do you need power? I am your power. Do you need wisdom? I am your wisdom. Do you need grace? I am your grace. Do you need fulness? I am your fulness. Just add in whatever you need. I AM."

"Tell them I AM has sent you, Moses. I AM the flame of fire in the thorn bush. The thorn bush has no life, no wisdom, no power, no grace, but I AM in the thorn bush everything that the thorn bush will need." It changed my whole understanding of the unmentionable name of God.

I believe that is exactly what John, a good Jew, was saying when he wrote the gospel of John. His gospel is an interpretation not a history, and he built it on eight signs and eight declarations. "I AM the bread of life. I AM the light of the world. I AM the door. I AM the good shepherd. I AM the resurrection and the life. Before Abraham was I AM. I AM the way, the truth, and the life. I AM the true vine." It is the unmentionable name of God.

This is the key to spiritual character. When you understand something of the I AM, then God begins to do something in your life. He can change you. He can change you into His likeness. He can develop a character in you. You become a character. Even some of us who have no natural character become real characters in the Lord. I did not say eccentric. Some of God's choicest saints are eccentric because they were eccentric when He saved them. And in one sense their very eccentricity reveals the Lord. But some people think that to be a character you have got to be odd. It does not. To be a real character, to have real character is just that through you the beauties of the Lord Jesus are touched and expressed.

When the dead, worthless thorn bush and the fire of God come together for good, God's purpose is fulfilled and history is made. That can be on your own personal level, family level, or fellowship level. This truth has been understood by many in the church, some with that gift of poetry. I think of Amy Carmichael. Here is one of her most beautiful little hymns:

> But I have seen a fiery flame
> Take to his pure and burning heart
> Mere dust of earth, to it impart
> His virtue, till that dust became
> Transparent loveliness of flame.

> O Fire of God, Thou fervent Flame,
> Thy dust of earth in thee would fall,
> And so be lost beyond recall,
> Transformed by Thee, its very name
> Forgotten in Thine own, O Flame.

Or I think of Margaret Barber. This is actually on this very verse: "Him that dwelt in the bush."

> In the wilderness for God!
> Just a common bush aflame!
> Thus may I be, Blessed Lord,
> For the glory of Thy Name.

Just a common bush to be,
Something in which God can dwell,
Something through which God can speak,
Something through which God can tell

All His yearning over men,
All His purposes of love.
Flaming with no light of earth,
But with glory from above:

God Himself within the bush,
Nothing seen but just the flame;
Make me that, just that, O God,
For the glory of Thy Name.

I have another one here that is my favorite because I always felt Charles Wesley was one of the greatest hymn writers in the history of the church.

O Thou who camest from above,
The pure celestial fire to impart,
Kindle a flame of sacred love
On the mean altar of my heart.

There let it for Thy glory burn
With inextinguishable blaze;
And trembling to its force return,
In humble prayer and fervent praise.

Jesus, confirm my heart's desire
To work, and speak, and think for Thee;
Still let me guard the holy fire,
And still stir up Thy gift in me.

Ready for all Thy perfect will,
My acts of faith and love repeat,
Till death Thy endless mercies seal,
And make the sacrifice complete.

Wesley understood something about this—make the sacrifice complete.

Enduring as I See Him

The second lesson I want to talk about—by the way all these overlap, all three of them—is the lesson of "enduring as seeing Him who is invisible." What an extraordinary phrase that is in Hebrews 11:27: "By faith Moses forsook Egypt, not fearing the Pharaoh, for he endured as seeing him who is invisible."

No child of God will ever endure anything unless he sees the invisible One. Let me put it another way. If Moses was to fulfill God's purpose, finish his course, keep the faith, he needed above all else endurance, perseverance, steadfastness.

If *you* are going to reach God's end in *your* life, if you are going to finish the course, run the race, keep the faith, obtain the crown, above all else you need endurance. You need that gift of perseverance. You need that gift of steadfastness.

One of the qualities that we do not see much in the twentieth century is endurance. Life is so easy, so affluent, so utilitarian, everything is instant, everything is done for you. There is not the same need to endure, the same need to persevere, the same need to be steadfast, but in spiritual things we have to endure if we are going to come to the end. It is so with your personal life. If God is going to do in you what He wants to do, you will have to know what it is to endure. It is the same with every family. What a tragedy it is if we believe in the salvation of God and have a family of unsaved children. No badgering of them, no pushing of them will ever bring them into the kingdom of God. In the end it is your character that will make the lasting impression upon your children. It is the fact that you not only teach but you live. And you will need to endure. Some of the finest servants of God have been the most rebellious children. We need the gift of endurance.

Do I need to say anything about the fellowship of God's people? The whole of the North American continent is littered with the ruins of church fellowship. Things that began with a great spirit, a great trumpet call, all excitement and emotion, within a few years are broken up and in disarray, disillusion, and disappointment. Very rarely do you ever find people who stay together. The most remarkable of all is whenever I find, anywhere in the world, leaders who have stayed together for years. Wherever I go I find leaders who have fallen out with one another and now can only bad mouth one another. It is amazing! The key to endurance is seeing Him who is invisible.

Let me put it another way. Do not be someone who looks *at* things; be a person who sees *through* things. Most people look at things. We see circumstances; they are physical, we think. We see situations; they are concrete, earthly, physical situations. We see difficult personalities; flesh and blood is all we see. If we only see these things, then we will do everything we can to change them or confront the personalities or manipulate the personalities or somehow get on top of those things. We need to see through to Him who is invisible. When we see through to the Lord a whole lot of new priorities come into our lives. We suddenly see the value and necessity of intercession. We suddenly see the tremendous importance of living faith when everything seems to be hopeless.

We need to see through all these things and see the Lord. Moses endured as seeing Him who is invisible. There is no difference with you or with me. This again is the burning bush. Do not see the bush; see the Lord. Do not stop with the thorns; see the flame of fire.

Let me put it another way. Christ-centeredness is the only key to endurance. It is only when you are centered on the Lord Jesus, taken up with the Lord Jesus, when you give Him the preeminence in everything in your life, only then can you endure. That ability to endure comes from Him. When you see the Lord, faith is created in your heart. When you see the Lord, you are changed into the same likeness. When you see the Lord, you get an understanding of your situation that you could never have apart from seeing the Lord. This is a tremendous lesson: "Enduring as seeing Him who is invisible."

Absolute Dependence on the Lord

My last lesson is the lesson of absolute dependence on the Lord. This is the same thing. It all comes out of this burning bush. We can learn from Moses this lesson of how he learned dependence on the Lord. The man of God becomes a man of God by dependence on the Lord. You do not become a man of God by reading books. They are important, but that is not the way you become a man of God. You do not become a man of God by just simply sitting in meetings. Meetings are important. We are told not to forsake the assembling of ourselves together, and so much the more as you see that day coming. But that is not the way you become a man of God. You become a man of God by learning to depend on the Lord. When you trust in yourself, you do not become a man of God. When you lean upon your own understanding, you do not become a man of God. It is exactly the same with the servant of the Lord. The servant of the Lord becomes a servant of the Lord by depending on the Lord. We cannot make someone a servant of the Lord. A servant of the Lord is produced by the Spirit of God. And how is such a servant produced? It is by dependence on the Lord.

You remember how Moses saw the Hebrew and Egyptian fighting, and we know that it was a taskmaster. It was one of the officers who was taking it out on one of the Hebrew slaves, and Moses said, "I am called to be the deliverer. This is where we begin." Now I do not know whether it is true, but our tradition says that Moses was a very strong man. He was a kind of spiritual Schwarzenegger because he was a military man. The princes of Egypt were specially trained. They had special diets and special exercises. We know that Moses was actually a hero in the military campaigns of Egypt. He was not some weak little creature. He was an unbelievably strong man, trained in martial arts, as well as in Egyptian learning. He not only had it in muscle, he had it in brains. Some people have got it in muscle and very little in brain. And some people have it in the brain and very little in muscle. But according to our tradition, Moses had both. Now he threw himself in. Had he not heard from his mother's lips that he had a special destiny? Had he not learned from his mother and father that maybe because of the unbelievable way that he had been drawn out of the River Nile he was to be the redeemer or deliverer of Egypt. Now he stepped in and threw down the taskmaster. How he did it we do not know. Was it a kind of kung fu chop? We do not know. But whatever he did, that taskmaster was out. Poor Moses may not have meant to go quite that far, but when he saw the man was dead, he buried him in the sand and told the Hebrew slave not to say a word. It was not dependence on the Lord. This was Moses' muscle power. This was Moses' ingenuity. This was Moses' brain working out how he could fulfill God's calling on his life. Don't we all fall into this?

God had to take him into the desert and for forty years drain him of all his natural energies, of his brainpower, and his muscle power, until finally he knew he was an exhausted, insignificant, dried up thorn bush. Then God said, "Now you are the thorn bush and I am the fire, and we shall be together."

The Presence of God

We have one marvelous summing up of this whole lesson in Exodus 33:14–15. When the Lord said to Moses, "My presence shall go with thee and I will give thee rest." And Moses said, "If your presence does not go with us, carry us not up hence."

In the Hebrew there is something you cannot put into English, and I can only put it in a very archaic way, but it may help you to understand. The accent is not on Moses. What the Lord said is this: "My presence will go, and I will give you rest." Of course it involved Moses moving, but the real thought is this: "It is not you go, Moses; I go with you. It is I go, you go with Me. When My presence moves, move with Me and you will get rest."

Have you noticed how many servants of God are worn out? How many come to a breakdown? What is it? Uncommanded works. I am guilty of it; we are all guilty of it. We get into doing things that the Lord has not told us to do and then there is not the grace and power available. The Lord does not give His grace and power for what He has not commanded. But when the Lord has commanded, then there is rest. Even in the busiest schedule, in the busiest and most exhausting work, there is rest. "My presence will go and I will give you rest." Then Moses said a very interesting thing: "If your presence does not go, do not let us go up." Oh, if we could learn this lesson of dependence upon the Lord! It is a tremendous lesson. Character is produced through learning to move with the Lord.

When I was young in the Lord I always used to wonder why Moses and Aaron, especially Moses, were always falling on their faces before the Lord. This phrase seemed very strange to me:

"And Moses fell on his face before the Lord." I thought, "Poor Moses, if he had a nose that is normally associated with our people. He was always falling flat on his face before the Lord." When I got to know the book a little more I used to think to myself: "Why does Moses always fall on his face before the Lord every time there is a problem?" This man knew the Lord face to face. This man was the friend of God. The Lord revealed His secrets to this man. He gave him the Law. After all, Moses is known all over the world as the lawgiver. It seemed so odd that every time there was a problem he did not look at what the Lord had given him, study it, and then apply it. He fell on his face before the Lord.

Now we make an enormous discovery in Christian work. We are all people who love to go by a book. Now don't get me wrong in this. We like to be legalists. We like to have a technique. How do you do it? Step one, step two, step three, step four, and then there is the result. Whether it is preaching, we are told to do this, this, and this. Whether it is healing, you do this, this, and this. Whether it is deliverance, you do this, this, this, and that. If it is getting you into an experience of the Spirit, you do this, this, and this. In some cases it works; in some it doesn't. When it does not work, we do not know what to do. To begin with we say, "There is something wrong with you. You better seek the Lord. There is some unbelief in your life or some sin in your life." We have a real problem with it. Sometimes it is the most godly people; that is the strange thing. Now we do not know quite what to do.

Nothing in the Book works without the living presence of God. I am a believer in the authority and inspiration and relevance of the Bible, and I mean by that all sixty-six books. I believe those strange genealogies are as important a part of God's word as anything that is more easily understandable. I do not believe there is anything in the Book that is irrelevant, nothing that is impractical, and nothing that is unnecessary, even though sometimes my brain does not fully understand why it is there. But having said that, I have to say that this Book does not work without the presence of the living God. It is when the Spirit of the Lord takes the Book and makes it live that something happens. You can know your Bible from end to end and not be born again. But when the Holy Spirit reveals something from the Book and it comes into the heart, in that moment you are born of God. And so it is with everything else.

When Moses fell on his face before the Lord, it was not that he did not know the Law God had given him. It was not even that he did not know perhaps what he should do. What he needed to find out from the Lord was how to do it and when to do it. This means that to be a servant of God you have to walk with the Lord. You have to keep in step with the Spirit of God. In other words, there cannot be anything that is just old, from years ago. We have to walk with the Lord now, dependent upon the Lord. We see it everywhere we look.

We have it in the New Testament in II Corinthians 4:7: "We have this treasure in earthen vessels that the exceeding greatness of the power may be of God and not from ourselves." And then it is almost as if he is describing Moses—pressed on every side, perplexed, pursued, smitten down. Perplexed, but not unto despair. Pressed on every side, yet not straitened. "Death in our body that the life also of Jesus may be manifested. So then death worketh in us [the thorn bush] and life in you." When we are too alive, *we* have life, and *you* get death. And when we are dead, you get life.

Sometimes the Lord has to take us very strange ways to bring us to the place where we are dependent on the Lord. The stronger we are in ourselves, the greater the discipline, the greater training of the Lord.

There could be no more important lessons from the life of Moses than these three. I have no idea how you see yourself. Maybe you thought you were the vine, and in one sense you are. Maybe you thought you were an olive branch, and so you should be. Maybe you thought you were that acacia wood in the house of the Lord, but until you recognize that you are nothing but an old, dead thorn bush, there is no possibility of the Lord putting the values into your life. Is it not sad that some of us have to wait to our deathbed before we finally realize that we are nothing and the Lord is everything?

May you take this, reflect on it, and meditate on it. Some people will take what I have said and make a tremendous amount about the thorn bush. This is the cross without the Spirit. Others will make a tremendous amount about the flame of fire, and this is the work and Person of the Holy Spirit. But it is the thorn bush and the fire together that are the key to fulfillment. May the Lord open our hearts and eyes, and may that flame of fire get into these old thorn bushes and never leave us. May the bush burn with fire and may the bush be not consumed.

Shall we pray?

Lord, only You can give us understanding of this kind of message. But in Your word You have spoken, dear Lord, about the eyes of our hearts being opened that we might understand, that we might know these things. We pray for that Spirit of wisdom and revelation in this matter. Help us, Lord. Help us to yield to You; help us to know You as fire, burning forever within us. And help us, Lord, in all the discipline and all the preparation that brings us to the place where we know our limitations, where we know what we are in ourselves, when we let go. Lord, will You work by Your Holy Spirit in us all, making us dependent upon Yourself, enabling us to endure as seeing Yourself who is invisible to our natural eyes. Hear us, Oh Lord, as we commit all this to you in the name of our Lord Jesus. Amen.

3.
The Prophet of God

Numbers 12:1–8

Cushite woman whom he had married; for he had married a Cushite woman. And they said, Hath the Lord indeed spoken only with Moses? hath he not spoken also with us? And the Lord heard it. Now the man Moses was very meek, above all the men that were upon the face of the earth.

And the Lord spake suddenly unto Moses, and unto Aaron, and unto Miriam, Come out ye three unto the tent of meeting.

And they three came out. And the Lord came down in a pillar of cloud, and stood at the door of the Tent, and called Aaron and Miriam; and they both came forth. And he said, Hear now my words: if there be a prophet among you, I the Lord will make myself known unto him in a vision, I will speak with him in a dream. My servant Moses is not so; he is faithful in all my house: with him will I speak mouth to mouth, even manifestly, and not in dark speeches; and the form of the Lord shall he behold: wherefore then were ye not afraid to speak against my servant, against Moses?

These lessons from the life of Moses have to do with spiritual character and service. We have these three ways in which Moses is described in the Bible. He is called the man of God. There could be no simpler title than that—the man of God, God's man. He is called the servant of the Lord, the Lord's servant. He is called the prophet of God, God's prophet. It is very interesting because in many ways you cannot really be a servant of the Lord unless first you are a man or woman of God. And it is the producing of spiritual character that in the end determines the quality of our service. When we come to leave this life, if the Lord does not return in our lifetime, then we leave everything behind. The only thing we take into eternity is what God has done in us. Sadly, there is not a lot of spiritual character among God's people. Most of the Lord's children are spectators and observers, seat warmers. They come into meetings and they just warm a seat. They listen, they judge the meeting, and they go out. There is so little, real spiritual character among God's children. And yet this matter of spiritual character is all-important.

We have already dealt with six lessons from the life of Moses. We have talked about the calling of God, total and costly commitment to the Lord, the principle of preparation, the key to all fulfillment, enduring as seeing Him who is invisible, and absolute dependence upon the Lord.

70 LESSONS FROM THE LIFE OF MOSES

Now I want to talk just a little, as the Lord helps me, about service. And I am very, very conscious that we need the enlightening work of the Holy Spirit. The first lesson I want to take is the producing of a servant of the Lord. I do not apologize for going over it. I think it has to be said again and again and again because somehow it does not always register with us the first time. Then I want to talk about the heart of Moses' service. What was he really called to do?

Producing a Servant of the Lord

Moses, the man of God, God's man, the man God, as it were, formed and prepared, becomes the servant of the Lord and God's prophet. Spiritual character determines our service. If there is little spiritual character, then our service will be superficial, it will be shallow, and it will be all to do with outward things. If the Lord can produce spiritual character in us of depth and quality, then the service we render will likewise have the same depth and the same quality. What are the essentials in serving God as we see in Moses?

Vision

The first absolute essential is vision. Nobody can serve the Lord unless the eyes of his heart have been opened. If we are spiritually blind, or we have spiritual problems with sight, it is very hard for us to serve the Lord acceptably. There are many, many problems with spiritual sight. Some people have long sight. They can only see what is coming in the far, far distance, and they have absolutely no vision for anything that is contemporary and at present. They walk as if they are living in the clouds.

Then there are those who are shortsighted. They can only see themselves or their families. They can hardly see beyond that even to the church, the building of the church. It is all to do with contemporary things.

Some people have double vision, and as a result they suffer from migraines, spiritual headaches. There are all kinds of eye diseases that God's people suffer from, but the absolute essential is to see the Lord. The God of glory appeared to our father Abraham while he was in Ur of the Chaldees in Mesopotamia. It changed Abraham's life. Abraham stepped into history; he made history. And I am not just talking about the history of this world. He made that as well, but actually he became an integral part of the fulfillment of God's purpose.

Jacob saw the Lord but Jacob had an enormous problem with himself. He had a super out-sized self-life. We all know that there are among us those who have super out-sized self-lives. They are an unbelievable problem to the church. When they get into the work of God, they tend to build empires. They tend to manipulate and influence people far and wide, but all the flaws and poison of the self-life are there. These folks that have a tremendous self-life are often very interesting and very attractive. But if the Lord cannot deal with us, then it destroys the very thing we want to see fulfilled. Don't we all know this in some way? We become the destroyer of the fulfillment of the very purpose of God we long to see fulfilled. We become the obstacles. Jacob is the great example of this. Oh, how he longed to be wholly for God! How he longed to have the birthright! How he longed to have the blessing! How he longed for the fulfillment of God's purpose! But his problem was himself—until he saw the Lord face to face. Here is the principle of vision.

Moses was the same—Moses, the prince, Moses, Pharaoh's daughter's son, Moses, who had all the physical advantages of learning, of training, of status, Moses who had understood from his father, Amram, and his mother, Jochabed, that God had a divine destiny and that he was going to be a deliverer, a redeemer of his people. Moses, till he saw the Lord, could only rely on himself. He could only rely on his own energy, his own gifts, his own talents, and his own background of education and training. But when he saw the Lord, it changed him.

We see it in the New Testament in the apostle Paul. He saw the Lord. In that vision of the Lord, he saw the church in embryonic form. This matter of vision is a principle with the Lord. If the Lord wanted to reveal His name I AM THAT I AM as being Almighty, Omnipresent, Omniscient, Creator of all things both in heaven and on earth, why didn't He use a tremendous, dramatic thunderstorm, with bolts of lightening, and rolls of thunder? Then while Moses was flat on his face He could have said to him, "My name is I AM THAT I AM."

I have been in storms in Israel, one of them twenty-six hours in duration, during which time it rolled with thunder and lightening the whole twenty-six hours. Another time I was in a storm for thirty hours. It began at eighty-six degrees Fahrenheit and ended with snow thirty hours later. If the Lord wanted to reveal the infinity of His Person, the almightiness of His power, His uncreatedness, why didn't He use a massive storm? I am not being irreverent I hope, may the Lord forgive me, but He crawled into a thorn bush. This is the most extraordinary thing. Think! The trouble with most Christians is that they do not think. They read these things and say, "Oh yes, the bush burned with fire and the bush was not consumed. And the Lord said, I AM THAT I AM. Isn't that amazing!" Oh, these wonderful sermons upon the infinity of God! Why did God get into a little dead thorn bush and meet with Moses? It was vision. Moses saw the Lord and was never the same again. Out of this vision, out of this seeing of the Lord, everything comes.

When the apostle writes that letter to the Ephesians, that greatest revelation of the eternal purpose of God in the whole Bible, before he goes on fully to explain all that he has begun to explain in the first chapter he says, "I must tell you what I am praying. I am praying to the God and Father of our Lord Jesus Christ that He will grant to you a spirit of wisdom and revelation in the knowledge of Him, that the eyes of your heart will be enlightened." It was as if Paul was frightened that the Ephesian letter would become material for theological seminaries, doctrine, or merely material for sermons. He wanted to let the church at Ephesus know that they needed the ministry of the Holy Spirit to open the eyes of their heart, that they might know not about the Lord Jesus, but that they might know what is the hope of His calling, and know what is the riches of the glory of His inheritance in the saints, and know what is the exceeding greatness of His power toward us. It is an absolute essential.

Now you may say to me, "Surely God's giving vision is sovereign." Yes, absolutely right. That is why the only way you and I will ever see the Lord in this way is when we are humble and seek Him. To the proud God reveals nothing. To the humble God reveals everything. This is the first absolute essential.

Living Faith

The second one is living faith. We never get faith by looking inside and trying to increase our faith. The devil comes to believers and says, "You cannot serve the Lord; you do not have enough faith. You must have a greater faith." "Oh," you say, "absolutely. I must have more faith." Now the devil has got you because he will say to you all the time, "Look in and investigate. What kind of faith have you got?" So you look inside and sort of investigate, and as you investigate your faith it shrivels before your eyes. It becomes smaller and smaller and smaller and smaller, until it is almost nonexistent. Then you become a kind of Christian cynic. And then the devil says, "I told you. Only those of great faith will see the mighty works of God." "Oh," you say, "yes, yes." Then the enemy says, "You better wait until you get more faith." And some of us wait a lifetime. It is not the amount of your faith; it is the functioning of the little faith you have. That is the thing that counts.

Jesus said in Matthew 17:20, "Verily, verily, I say unto you, If you have faith as a grain of mustard seed." A grain of mustard seed! With so little faith you can move mountains. Why then do we need this kind of living faith? If we see the Lord and we see the greatness of the Lord and the power of the Lord and understand that we are just a dead old thorn bush but the I AM is in us, nothing is impossible. Nothing is impossible! Then you are joined to the

Creator of the universe, then you are one with the All-Powerful, then you have been made one with God Himself.

"By faith, Moses..." It says it three times in Hebrews 11. Here is a second absolute essential in serving the Lord. If you and I are going to be servants of the Lord, we need living faith. Praise the Lord, when we see the Lord, faith is a spontaneous response. It is an amazing thing; it is always the same.

I think of Peter in the boat at sea. Jesus deliberately did not get in the boat with him, and then a great storm came up. It is an interesting thing that once before the Lord was with them in the boat when a great storm came, and they all panicked. They left Him asleep while they bailed out the water. Unbelievable! Then they finally woke Him and said, "We are perishing." The Lord realized they were panic-stricken and the only thing He could do was say, "Sh-h-h-h", and the whole thing stopped.

The second time He made sure He was not in the boat. A storm hit the ship and the Lord was not in the boat. They were rowing hard against the storm, wondering whether they were going to make it at all because those storms in the lake of Galilee are very sudden and very dramatic and powerful. Suddenly, through the mist and spray and the great rollers, they thought they saw a ghost. Then Peter said, "I think it is the Lord." So he yelled out through the roar of the wind and the waves:

"Is it You, Jesus?"

And Jesus said, "Yes, it is Me."

Then Peter said, "Well, if it is You, tell me to come." And Jesus said, "Come." Peter got out of the boat and walked on the water. Now this was not a placid, mirror-like lake, beautiful, just like ice. It was a roaring sea with great waves. And Peter got up and walked on it. He did the impossible. It is the most amazing thing. He did not even think about it. He saw the Lord; he heard the Lord; he obeyed the Lord, and living faith worked. He walked up and down the waves. That's how I see it. Up and down, up and down he went. Every one thinks that there was this wonderful mirror-like sea and Jesus saying, "Come." It is a miracle even if he walked on calm water. But it was not calm; it was a storm.

Peter had never been to theological seminary and learned how to walk on the water. He had never had a course with Jesus in the four steps to walking on the sea. He had never done such a thing in his life. He knew there was a law of gravity even if he could not explain it in such terms. And yet there he was walking on water. How do you explain it? "Oh," you say, "he had tremendous faith." No, he did not. He saw the Lord, he heard the Lord, and faith was the automatic, spontaneous response. He did the impossible. It is an amazing thing. If we could only see this we would not ask for more faith. We would ask to see the Lord; we would ask to hear the Lord. Then we would do the impossible, for the more we see of the greatness of the Lord, and the power of the Lord, and the faithfulness of the Lord, the more we shall walk on the stormy sea. Then I imagine a great wave came by with a great roar, and suddenly Peter could not see the Lord. A wave came between him and the Lord and all he could think was, "What am I doing? I am walking on the sea." Immediately he sank.

I shall never forget what one liberal told us: "Now we all know Jesus was walking in shallow water, ankle deep." So someone asked him, "How did Peter sink in this ankle deep water?" And he said, "He fell into a pot hole." Such are the explanations of those who try to make the Bible explicable. Their explanations require more faith than the word itself.

Anyway, Peter began to sink and immediately the Lord took hold of him and said, "Why did you doubt, oh ye of little faith?" This matter of living faith is all-important. It is the only way you and I will ever become a servant of the Lord. It is the only way you and I will ever serve the Lord. Do you think that we are going to be able to serve the Lord with an enemy such as we have? With the powers of darkness ranged against us? Do you think that we are going to be able to serve the Lord when sometimes within our hearts lurks that awful unbelief that the enemy can play upon and beam his propaganda machine to? We need living faith. It is the second essential.

Absolute Obedience

Absolute obedience is the third essential. (All these are overlapping of course; you understand that.) When God has a servant, He wants obedience. It is the one thing you require in a servant. If a servant cannot obey, what is the point of being a servant? A servant is someone who obeys, and this matter of absolute obedience is of tremendous importance.

It is a wonderful thing about Moses; he did everything the Lord told him to do. He argued with the Lord. He tried to get out of certain things by excusing himself this way or another. But in fact, dear Moses did everything he was ever commanded but one thing. Only one thing is recorded in which he disobeyed the Lord—when he lost his temper. The Lord had told him to lift up his rod and speak to the rock and command the water to come out. And Moses lost his temper with that unruly, rebellious, critical, murmuring crowd of believers and whacked the rock twice and said, "You rebels, do I have to bring water out of this rock?" It was the only time he disobeyed the Lord. And because this principle of absolute obedience is so important the Lord would not allow Moses to enter the land. He has become for us a very serious example, an illustration of disobedience and its consequences. Isn't that is a beautiful phrase in Numbers 12 and Hebrews 3? "Moses was faithful in all his house."

Meekness

The fourth essential is meekness. This is something that falls very strangely upon twentieth century ears. Latter twentieth century folks generally understand meekness as weakness. Moses was anything but weak. He was physically strong, and intellectually strong. Moses was a strong personality, a strong man. Why does it say he was the meekest man on the face of all the earth? What is meekness? I believe that we get a key to meekness in the New Testament. It is in Matthew 11:29–30: "Take My yoke upon you, and learn of Me; for I am meek and lowly in heart: and ye shall find rest unto your souls. For My yoke is easy, and My burden is light."

I understand from this comment of our Lord Jesus that meekness is to be teachable. Meekness is to be, as it were, open to the Lord: "Learn of Me for I am meek and lowly in heart." Then He goes on to say, "You will not only find rest to your souls but you will find My yoke is easy and My burden is light."

Meekness is something tremendously important as I see it. In Exodus 33:13, Moses says, "Now therefore, I pray thee, if I have found favor in thy sight, show me now thy ways." Do you know the comment of the Psalmist on this? Listen to Psalm 103: "He made known his ways unto Moses, His acts unto the children of Israel."

I am not being unkind, but I want to put it this way to bring it home to you. Any fool can see the acts of the Lord, but to understand the ways of the Lord, that requires an open, inquiring, seeking, teachable spirit. A servant of the Lord is not some autocrat. He is not some petty dictator. He is not some great authority. A servant of the Lord derives all of his authority from the Lord. Without the Lord he has no authority. He is nothing without the Lord. He is a dried up, dead old thorn bush. That is all! But if the flame of fire is in the bush, *there* is the authority of God, *there* is the power of God, *there* is the wisdom of God, *there* is the life of God, and *there* is the fulness of God. It is all there in the Lord in the flame of fire in the bush.

Here then is meekness. Do you think the Lord will take those who are proud, who are arrogant, who are self-sufficient in their knowledge, who throw their weight around? Of course not! This is the tragedy of church life. We have so many people throwing their weight around, so many authoritarians, so many who are, in themselves, something. They are the wreckers of the church.

I am all for signs and wonders, personally. I do not know what it is about some of the Lord's children; they are frightened to death of a miracle. It is as if the only miracles that ever took place were in the Bible. If you have never had a miracle in your life, I am sorry for you. I had a miracle in my life; I got converted.

That was the fundamental miracle. And if God can do such a miracle and save a person like me and bring me to new birth in Himself and make me alive to God, I believe God can do anything. I am sorry for people who have never had a miracle in their life. But God does not stop at one miracle; He goes on and on—signs and wonders—I am not afraid of signs and wonders, but the trouble is that so many of the Lord's people get so excited with the outward. They are so excited with the signs and wonders, they do not even see what it signifies. They are just thrilled with the actual power in the miracle. To know the ways of the Lord, that is something for eternity; to see the acts of God that may only be for time. Meekness therefore is the fourth absolute essential in this whole matter.

Absolute Dependence upon the Lord

The fifth essential is absolute dependence upon the Lord. What can a dried up thorn bush do? You stuff it in your stove and it will keep the fire going for precisely a minute. What can you do with a thorn bush? With grapes you can make wine, with figs you can get sweetness and a lot of health-giving properties, with pomegranates, you can get iron. There are lots of things you can do with all these things, but what can you do with a dried up old thorn bush? You cannot change a nation; you cannot bring a nation to birth; you cannot fulfill the purpose of God. Have you ever heard of such a thing?

What can a thorn bush do? But what can the I AM in the thorn bush not do? When the I AM is in the thorn bush, there is *nothing* impossible. The whole purpose of God through your life can be fulfilled. The whole purpose of God for His people can be fulfilled. History can be made. Situations can be changed. Lives can be influenced for eternity. Families can be saved. The impossible can be done because the I AM is in the bush. Some people get so thrilled about the work of the cross, and it is something to get thrilled about, painful as it is. But then without even knowing it they put such an emphasis on the dried up old thorn bush that somehow or other they forget that the thorn bush is nothing. You cannot do anything with a thorn bush. Think of a congregation of dried up old thorn bushes! What can you do with them? But if the I AM is in the thorn bush, if the fire is in the thorn bush, anything can happen.

So this matter of total dependence upon the Lord is tremendous. It is a painful thing to be brought to an end, because our natural fallen nature is to find self-sufficiency. It is to find our sufficiency within ourselves, to develop our talents, to train our gifts, to consecrate our energies. The church has never suffered so much as it has from the gifts of its members. It is our gifts. Here is a brother who can organize. Let him get to work and any movement of the Spirit will be destroyed within two years. He will organize it so perfectly that it will die. Here is a person with tremendous natural charisma. Let him loose on the people of God and they will all be taken in by him. He will build an empire and before long fleece them of their money. We cannot help it. No one starts this way. No one is so malicious and wicked as to start out and thinks, "I am going to fool them all and take their money." It is the natural charisma of the self-life, and once it begins to work you are carried along with an Amazon-like flood;

you cannot stop it. When you see people are easily influenced and duped, then comes the contention.

Wouldn't it be lovely if all we had to say was, "I am going to be dependent on the Lord"? Do you know what you are saying? "Oh," you say, "yes, yes, yes; I am going to be dependent on the Lord. I understand now what you have said. If I am dependent on the Lord I shall see the purpose of God for my life fulfilled, the purpose of God for my family fulfilled, the purpose of God in the fellowship of God's people fulfilled." Do you know what you are saying? You are asking God to reduce you to a thorn bush. You are asking God to start to take hold of your circumstances and situations and bring you into things that are beyond you, to bring you into situations that are so impossible that *your* gifts and energies die a natural death.

The Servant and His Service Are One

The sixth thing is the identification of the servant with his service, the identification of the prophet with his ministry. In real service the servant of the Lord and his service are one. Your service will come out of your servanthood. In other words, what the Lord is doing in you is what will come out in your service. Let me put it another way for those who are more charismatic. If you speak in a tongue and you have no spiritual character, your tongue will be pretty frothy. "Oh, that is not right," you say. "If the Spirit of the Lord manifests Himself it will be tremendous even if I am shallow." No, it will not. That is occultism. That is this idea that when the Spirit of the Lord comes upon you, He suspends all that you are and uses you as a kind of puppet. Nonsense!

This is occultism. I have used tongues as an example because I know some people are going to get steamed up on this one. Or let's take faith. Whatever gift it is, whatever you are comfortable with, if there is little of the Lord in you, there will be little of the Lord in the gift. There is not the capacity. But if the Lord can work a deep, full capacity in your life for the I AM, as it were, to express Himself, then the depths will come out. Unsearchable riches will begin to come through your life.

If you look at some of these prophets and these great servants of God in the old covenant and the new, you will see that the Lord takes their ministry and He makes them one with their ministry. He did the strangest things with some of these prophets. Think of poor Hosea. What an extraordinary thing the Lord did with him! He married a very faithless woman, and the Lord told him to do it. Why? because Israel was faithless. That seems very strange.

Or think of Ezekiel. When his wife died, the Lord said, "Don't you mourn." Different from Moses, Ezekiel had a very happy marriage according to our tradition, but when his wife died, the Lord said to him, "Don't mourn." That is a very strange thing to do. How hard it was for Ezekiel!

If you truly want to serve the Lord, if you want to become a servant of God, one who is a contributing factor in His work and among His people, there is a principle here. He will make you one with your service. It will either come out of your experience or you will have the experience after you have spoken. But the Lord will be faithful in this matter.

The Preparation of the Holy Spirit

The seventh essential is the preparation and training of God's Holy Spirit. Forty years preparation in the desert: that was Moses' experience—the rod, the hand, the water of the river. At the end of those forty years, when God had reduced him to a dried up, dead thorn bush, then Moses could not even consider going. He said, "It is no good, Lord. I stutter."

The Lord had to humor him; He said, "That is all right, take Aaron." And ever afterwards Moses did the speaking and Aaron did the acting. It is very strange. And yet the Lord had to humor him and say, "All right, take Aaron. He will do the talking." The Lord had done such a good job in Moses, now he could not even get him moving.

The Rod

Then Moses said, "But they will say, 'The Lord did not appear to you.'"

Then He said, "What is that in your hand?"

"A rod."

Now this rod was the thing that all the way through the life of Moses he was to use again and again and again. The Lord said to him, "Throw it on the ground."

Suddenly the rod became a snake, but not just one of those harmless snakes. I do not like snakes. I find it very strange when people wrap them around their necks. I had a friend who had a twenty-foot python and never told me it was in the room next to me. I went to stay with him and there it was in the next room. I was horrified when I heard. I do not like them. I know some people say they are lovely. I was with a friend in a shop that had great big tarantulas. (We have tarantulas in Israel, dreadful things.) And he said, "Charming little fellow, I think I will buy it." And I said, "Not while I am with you." I cannot believe that people could have this kind of pet. I have many pets at home, dogs and cats and cockatoos (parrots), but no snakes.

He threw down the rod and it did not become just a harmless snake; it was a sand viper. Moses fled. He had been a shepherd for forty years. He knew all about sand vipers. As soon as he saw it, he was out. He knew the thing was angry. He would never have thrown down that rod if he had known it was a snake. The thing was angry. It had enough intelligence to come after him. Then the Lord said, "Moses, come back. Take up this snake by its tail." You all know you never take a snake up by its tail unless it is a certain kind of snake, but certainly not a sand viper. You just do not do it. It will curl round and sting you, and you have had it. You will be a hospital case if they get you in time.

But there is Moses, meekly obeying the Lord. Oh, what a man of God! He takes that snake up by the tail and it becomes a rod. Moses understood from this that in his ministry and service there was the poison of hell. It was within his self-life. Until he let go of that self-life and laid it down, he did not know what was in it. But the moment he let go of it and laid it down, he saw the real nature of Satan within his self-life. It would destroy his ministry, destroy his service. He saw it and he understood. Then, it is as if he had such a revulsion, he was so repelled that he did not want to touch his self-life again. Then the Lord said, "Take it up. Take it up by faith."

The Hand

It is the same with the hand. The hand is the thing that you do everything with. After all, his hand was holding the rod. Now the Lord said, "Put your hand in your bosom." It is the heart. This is where all your feelings are, the most intimate part of your being. Do you know there is leprosy there? Out came his hand, not just slightly leprous, but white; it was advanced leprosy. "Put it back in." He put it back in and took it out. It was clean. What was the Lord saying to him? Surely the Lord was saying, "Moses, I have reduced you to a thorn bush. You have finally understood the power of Satan in self-centered flesh."

The River

What about the river? The Lord said, "If any do not understand these two things, then take the water of the river." Of course in our phraseology we always speak of *the* river. We have the River Jordan in Israel; it is a little stream. When I travel to the States and see these huge rivers, I ask what the name of that river is. The people who live near it do not even know, and it is about ten times the size of the River Jordan. Jordan is a tiny little stream. Wherever the Bible says *the* river, it is the Nile. Now the Lord said, "Take of the water of *the* river." I have flown over Egypt and seen that amazing triangle of emerald green in the midst of thousands of miles desert. On one side is the Arabian; on the other side is the Sahara. It is unbelievable to see it. Wherever that river goes it is emerald green, but it is Egyptian. The Nile is an Egyptian River, and Egypt is always a picture of the world. So what is the Lord saying? Water is always a picture of life, but it is our self-life; it is our fallen life; it is our flesh-life. Take it up, pour it on the dry ground, and it will become blood. Through the atoning work of the Lord Jesus that natural life of yours will become, as it were, the resurrection life of the Lord Jesus. This is preparation and training.

Genuine Leadership

The last essential is genuine leadership. There are so few leaders. There are thousands of seeming leaders, but there are so few real leaders. I always remember Austin-Sparks saying, "A leader is a pioneer." In the Israeli Army we have something that is quite unique to us. Our captains, our officers lead us, and the most common little phrase is, "Follow me." You do not get this in the British Army. You are told to go forward and the officers stay back in safety. And I believe it is so with the American Army as well. The whole mentality of the West is that the officers stay back and the men go forward. "Forward!" It is not, "Follow me!" It is, "Forward!" In the work of the Lord, the leaders are first. They are pioneers, and they should be examples of everything. They should be able to say, "Follow me." In the question of authority, it is to manifest the authority of the Lord Jesus. It is to become a vehicle for the mind and heart of God. That is producing a servant.

The Service of Moses

The service of Moses, that to which he was essentially called, was related to two matters. First of all, it was the law of God or the word of God. Second, it was the tabernacle of God or God's dwelling place. To these two matters Moses' whole service was related. Isn't it so? All the rest are peripheral. If we are talking about essential service, it is the word of God and the tabernacle, the law of God and the tabernacle.

The Law of God

What is this law of God? It is the Ten Words. We say in Hebrew in our tradition "The Ten Words." You say in the Christian tradition "The Ten Commandments." This is the heart. You will find it from Exodus 20—24. In that Ark of the Covenant was an unbroken Ten Words. There can be no salvation without a Savior who kept, unbroken, the Ten Words.

Second, from these Ten Words we have a tremendous amount more in explanation and interpretation in Leviticus, Numbers, and Deuteronomy. So, we have first the Ten Words; that is the heart. Then, we have all this other that comes out in interpretation and explanation. And then we have beyond even this the Law or Torah of God. In our tradition when we say Torah of Moses or the Torah of God, we do not just mean the Ten Commandments nor do we just mean the Levitical commandments. We mean the whole five books—Genesis, Exodus, Leviticus, Numbers, and Deuteronomy. This is the Torah of God; this is the Law of Moses. Everything in the Bible is built on these first five books that came to us through the editorship of Moses as well as the actual writing of Moses. They are the foundation of the whole Bible. Don't listen to this absolute nonsense that is taught in some parts of the Christian Church that they are nothing. If you do away with the first five books of the Bible, you have taken out the lynchpin of the whole Bible. You have destroyed your Bible. That is how Satan, in the whole higher criticism movement, liberalism in Germany, destroyed the faith of the German Church in the Bible by attacking the first five books of the Bible.

I could talk about "J" and "E" and "P" and all these ridiculous theories that have dominated theology for nearly a hundred and twenty or thirty years, and now our Hebrew philologists and experts, professors in Hebrew, cannot find a single evidence for this theory. And the whole of Christian theology has been built on "J" and "E" and "JE" and "P." "J" is Jehovah; everybody who finds Jehovah is one source. Everybody who finds God Elohim is another source. Jehovah Elohim is another source, and "P" is the Priestly. Isn't it stupid? They have destroyed our Bible and destroyed the foundation upon which everything is built.

All the historical books of the Old Testament, all the wisdom books of the Old Testament, all the prophetic books of the Old Testament grow out of the first five books of the Bible. The whole twenty-seven writings of the New Testament grow out of these five books. There is not a single doctrine of the twenty-seven writings in the New Testament that is not founded in origin in the first five books of the Bible.

So we have Moses and the word of God. No wonder Satan wanted Moses. You know Satan was so mad over Moses that when he was dead he wanted his dead body. The archangel Michael had to contend for the dead body of Moses (see Jude 9). Isn't it amazing? Satan so hated this man and everything this man stood for because this man was a vehicle for God to bring something to the whole world—the foundation of the whole word of God. All Moses' service, all his deliverance, all his calling, all his preparation, all of his being reduced to a thorn bush so that he would know the I AM in him, was related to the word of God—the coming of the word of God, the giving of the word of God, this foundational five books of the sixty-six books of the Bible.

The Tabernacle

The second thing to which Moses' service is related is the tabernacle. God revealed to him the whole tabernacle in precise detail. Why is God so bothered about this? He tells him that these boards are to be such and such a length; they are to be shot through this way. He gives all the measurements, all the details. He tells them exactly what kind of curtains there should be, where the gold should be, what kind of wood it should be. What is the Lord doing? Is the Lord so interested in a little tent? He does not leave a single thing to Moses' imagination, as our dear liberal theologians tell us: "Moses' was affected by the Egyptians. The tabernacle was really an Egyptian thing." I have never seen anything like it in Egypt. They have pyramids and sphinxes. It seems to me the Egyptians went in for something monumental, something in stone, something that lasted. Here is God saying, "I want to dwell among this people. I AM. I want to be in the thorn bush. You must make me a tabernacle that I may dwell in it. This tabernacle is found in Exodus 25—40. You will find it again and again mentioned in various ways in Numbers, Leviticus, and Deuteronomy.

We have a most interesting phrase in the New Testament. We are told in Hebrew 8:4 that it is the shadow of heavenly things. In chapter 9:4 we are told it is the pattern of the truth.

So Moses was not just setting up a little tent with two compartments, with various pieces of furniture, and an outer court. It was a shadow of heavenly things. It was a pattern of the real, of the eternal.

It is interesting that when that tabernacle was set up, for the first time the glory of God touched the earth. You all remember the dictum that whenever something is first mentioned in the Bible, it is very important. Here we have the first mention of the glory of God touching the earth. Where did the glory of God come into the tabernacle? What did it do? It filled the whole tent with His presence. Nobody could stand to minister. Isn't that amazing? What does it speak of? Surely it speaks of the house of God. Surely it speaks of the temple of God, the home of God in the Spirit.

The Passover lamb is the origin. When we have the Passover lamb, we have the unbroken Ten Words, then we have the dwelling place of God. It is Jesus— the Lamb, the fulfilled law of God, the dwelling place of God. "The Word became flesh and dwelt among us, and we beheld His glory, glory as of the only begotten of the Father, full of grace and truth." The Passover lamb, the unbroken Law of God, the dwelling place of God, and the glory of God—we have the whole Bible here.

The Word of God and the Testimony of Jesus

It is of enormous significance that in the last book of the Bible, Revelation, we have a phrase that is hardly found anywhere else in the Bible. We have one little intimation in the first Corinthian letter and that is all. This phrase is only found in the book of Revelation: "the word of God and the testimony of Jesus" In some wonderful way Moses was related to the word of God and the testimony of Jesus. No wonder it says in one place in Revelation that "they sing the song of Moses, the servant of God and the song of the Lamb." He was somehow related to this.

Here we have the key to world history. The focal point of all the conflict is the "word of God and the testimony of Jesus." All through history the powers of darkness have one way or another sought to contradict the word of God, frustrate the word of God in its fulfillment, and stop the testimony of Jesus from ever coming. They have failed, but if I understand my Bible correctly, in the last phase of world history the final attempt of the enemy to destroy the word of God and the testimony of Jesus will take place. We are very, very near to it, and do not think that in the States you are going to escape. Something terrible is taking place in American society, something foundational. I only visit Britain once a year, and therefore as a kind of spectator and observer, I am shocked when I walk through the streets of the town that I grew up in, a high class area of England, to see brutalized faces. I have never seen it before except in the Nazis. It is the beginning of a demonic influence, the beginning of demonic possession of ordinary human beings. It is going to come to the States, if it is not already here. The focal point of the whole last conflict as recorded in the book of Revelation is on "the word of God and the testimony of Jesus."

The Word of God

Now what does "the word of God" mean to us? I think of the words of the apostle Paul to his son in the faith, Timothy. He says in II Timothy 3:15–17, "And that from a babe thou hast known the sacred writings which are able to make thee wise unto salvation through faith which is in Christ Jesus. All scripture is inspired of God and is profitable for teaching, for reproof, for correction, for instruction which is in righteousness: that the man of God may be complete, furnished completely unto every good work."

In other words, if the man of God is to be complete, the Holy Spirit has to take the word of God and bring it into us. The word of God has somehow or other to become flesh and blood in us by the work of the Holy Spirit, that the man of God (Moses, the man of God) may be complete, furnished completely unto every good work—the servant of the Lord, the prophet of God. How? It is by the word of God. Don't treat the word of God cheaply. Don't treat it in a familiar way. The whole of our society is moving away from the Judeo-Christian revelation that God has given. It is moving away medically, scientifically, socially, and religiously. It is finding other concepts, new foundations. This means that you and I really need to hold the word of God. We need to study it. We need to seek the Lord for illumination. We need to ask the Lord for wisdom if we lack it. We really need to call upon the Lord that He will make us those who are living epistles or letters of God.

In this matter of the word of God, a subtle and terrible change is taking place in the Christian church. When I say the Christian church I am not talking about the nominal, the liberal, or what I call the unsaved church. I am talking about those who know God. People are no longer subject to the word of God. They subject the word of God to themselves. Once we subject the word of God to ourselves, then we manipulate it, change it, make it more adaptable to modern concepts and fashions. We try to make it mean something else that nobody has ever seen in the last four thousand years. The best example is what the Methodists have done with the alternative Lord's Prayer: "Our Mother, who art in heaven, hallowed be thy name." As if any real believer ever thought that there was no female principle in the Godhead. It is absolutely ridiculous! It is all because of modern concepts, and it will be the destruction of the church. It will be the beginning of the apostasy, the beginning of the falling away. We need to be subject to the word of God. We may not understand all the word of God, and it may not always make sense to us, but we have to accept that the word of God is the word of God. We must be subject to it. Remember that "the word of God is living and active and sharper than any two-edged sword, dividing between soul and spirit."

The Testimony of Jesus

What is the testimony of Jesus? I will take one thing in the context of all that I have already said: the old thorn bush and the I AM. Now take John's gospel. "I AM the bread of life ... I AM the light of the world. He that followeth me shall not walk in darkness but shall have the light of life ... Before Abraham was I AM ... I AM the door ... I AM the good shepherd ... I AM the resurrection and the life. He that believeth on Me though he were dead yet shall he live, and he that liveth and believeth on Me shall never die ... I AM the way, the truth and the life. No man cometh unto the Father but by Me. ... I AM the true vine."

It is interesting he begins with bread and ends with the vine. He begins with the personal and ends with the corporate. The vine has always been a symbol for the Jewish people of the nation. And when Jesus said, "I AM the true vine, my Father is the husbandman," He was actually saying, "I AM the nation. I AM the church," if you want to put it that way. "Abide in Me and I in you." We are branches in the vine bearing fruit. This is the testimony of Jesus.

Is it not interesting at the very end of the Bible, in Revelation 19, the fellow servant says to John, "For the testimony of Jesus is the spirit of prophecy." In other words, the very nature of the church and holding the testimony of Jesus is prophetic. It is the revelation in a contemporary way of the mind and heart of God.

When I come to the very last chapters of the Bible, Revelation 21—22, I see a bride; I see a New Jerusalem; I see the city of God coming down out of heaven having the glory of God. Then I hear the most amazing declaration: "There is no need of sun or moon in this city, for the glory of God does lighten it, and the Lamb is the lamp thereof." Then what is the stand? The city is the stand. The Lamb is the lamp, and the glory of God is the light. This is the testimony of Jesus. If we have to be strictly, technically, theologically correct, the testimony of Jesus, in my estimation, is not the church, although the testimony of Jesus is the church. The testimony of Jesus is what we hold in the church, so that the church can go on, but the lampstand can be removed.

I do not have any doubt that this will be the last great battle. The focal point of tremendous battle will be the nature of the church, the gathering together of people of the Lord. It is a tremendous comfort to me that in this same book of Revelation, in the midst of all the conflict and all the battle we suddenly hear a cry. And this cry is not some small cry; it is like the waters of the sea, like mighty thunders: "Hallelujah! The Lord God the Almighty reigns. Let us rejoice and be exceeding glad, for the marriage of the Lamb is come and the bride has made herself ready."

So we know from the word of God that it is going to happen. If only in a remnant all over the world, there will be those who are faithful to God, who will commit themselves wholly to God, and will go the whole way with the Lord. By the grace of God I want to be part of that bride. I am sure you do too.

Here is the service of Moses. Here is a lesson that is tremendous—the word of God and the testimony of Jesus. This is the focal point, not only of the conflict; it is the focal point of our service—to hold the word of God and the testimony of Jesus. May He help us.

Shall we pray:

Lord, we need Your help. We need Your illumination. Lord, there may be many things said this evening we have not quite got or understood, but Lord, by Your Spirit reveal them to us. Make them a living reality to every one of us. We know we are moving now into tremendous days of conflict, of change, and of spiritual and moral darkness, the beginning of the rise of the antichrist. Will You help us, Lord, to be clear on the issues, and help us to follow You fully to the end. We look for Your appearing, Lord. Let that hope of Your coming purify us, refine us, and make us those who are prepared to be men and women of God, servants of Yours serving You. We ask it in the name of our Lord Jesus. Amen.

4.
The Intercessor

Numbers 14:11–19

And the Lord said unto Moses, How long will this people despise me? and how long will they not believe in me, for all the signs which I have wrought among them? I will smite them with the pestilence, and disinherit them, and will make of thee a nation greater and mightier than they.

And Moses said unto the Lord, Then the Egyptians will hear it; for thou broughtest up this people in thy might from among them; and they will tell it to the inhabitants of this land. They have heard that thou Lord art in the midst of the people; for thou Lord art seen face to face, and thy cloud standeth over them, and thou goest before them, in a pillar of cloud by day, and in a pillar of fire by night. Now if thou shall kill this people as one man, then the nations which have heard the fame of thee will speak, saying, Because the Lord was not able to bring this people into the land which he sware unto them, therefore he hath slain them

---

*in the wilderness. And now, I
pray thee, let the power of the
Lord be great, according as thou
hast spoken, saying, the Lord
is slow to anger, and abundant
in lovingkindness, forgiving
iniquity and transgression; and
that will by no means clear the
guilty, visiting the iniquity of
the fathers upon the children,
upon the third and upon the
fourth generation. Pardon, I
pray thee, the iniquity of this
people according unto the
greatness of thy lovingkindness,
and according as thou hast
forgiven this people, from Egypt
even until now.*

Exodus 33:12–19

*And Moses said unto the Lord,
See, thou sayest unto me, Bring
up this people: and thou hast
not let me know whom thou wilt
send with me. Yet thou hast said,
I know thee by name, and thou
hast also found favor in my*

*sight. Now therefore, I pray thee,
if I have found favor in thy sight,
show me now thy ways, that I
may know thee, to the end that
I may find favor in thy sight:
and consider that this nation
is thy people. And he said, My
presence shall go with thee, and
I will give thee rest. And he said
unto him, If thy presence go not
with me, carry us not up hence.
For wherein now shall it be
known that I have found favor
in thy sight, I and thy people? is
it not in that thou goest with us,
so that we are separated, I and
thy people, from all the people
that are upon the face of the
earth?*

*And the Lord said unto
Moses, I will do this thing also
that thou hast spoken; for thou
hast found favor in my sight,
and I know thee by name. And
he said, Show me, I pray thee,
thy glory. And he said, I will
make all my goodness pass*

*before thee, and will proclaim
the name of the Lord before thee;
and I will be gracious to whom I
will be gracious, and will show
mercy on whom I will show
mercy.*

Deuteronomy 32:48–52

*And the Lord spake unto Moses
that selfsame day, saying, Get
thee up into this mountain
of Abarim, unto mount Nebo,
which is in the land of Moab,
that is over against Jericho;
and behold the land of Canaan,
which I give unto the children
of Israel for a possession; and
die in the mount whither thou
goest up, and be gathered
unto thy people, as Aaron thy
brother died in mount Hor,
and was gathered unto his
people: because ye trespassed
against me in the midst of the
children of Israel at the waters
of Meribah of Kadesh, in the
wilderness of Zin; because ye*

*sanctified me not in the midst of
the children of Israel. For thou
shalt see the land before thee;
but thou shalt not go thither
into the land which I give the
children of Israel.*

Deuteronomy 34:1–12

*And Moses went up from the
plains of Moab unto mount
Nebo, to the top of Pisgah, that
is over against Jericho. And
the Lord showed him all the
land of Gilead, unto Dan, and
all Naphtali, and the land of
Ephraim and Manasseh, and
all the land of Judah, unto the
hinder sea, and the South and
the Plain of the valley of Jericho
the city of palm-trees, unto Zoar.
And the Lord said unto him,
This is the land which I sware
unto Abraham, unto Isaac, and
unto Jacob, saying, I will give
it unto thy seed: I have caused
thee to see it with thine eyes, but
thou shalt not go over thither.*

So Moses the servant of the Lord died there in the land of Moab, according to the word of the Lord. And he buried him in the valley in the land of Moab over against Beth-peor: but no man knoweth of his sepulchre unto this day. And Moses was a hundred and twenty years old when he died: his eye was not dim, nor his natural force abated. And the children of Israel wept for Moses in the plains of Moab thirty days: so the days of weeping in the mourning for Moses were ended. And Joshua the son of Nun was full of the spirit of wisdom; for Moses had laid his hands upon him: and the children of Israel hearkened unto him, and did as the Lord commanded Moses. And there hath not arisen a prophet since in Israel like unto Moses, whom the Lord knew face to face, in all the signs and the wonders, which the Lord sent him to do in the land of Egypt, to Pharaoh, and to all his servants, and to all his land, and in all the mighty hand, and in all the great terror, which Moses wrought in the sight of all Israel.

I want to take four more lessons from the life of Moses. Each one is very important and very significant in this matter of spiritual character and true and genuine service. All of these lessons we are learning from the life of Moses overlap. You cannot categorize them as being totally unrelated to one another.

Intercession

The first lesson, in my estimation, is the heart of God in Moses. I think it is wonderful that Moses got to this position in the end. I would very simply describe this lesson as Moses, the intercessor. Intercession is the crown of all service. It is the deepest form of ministry that any servant of God can offer. It is a tragedy that this word *intercession* is devalued among the people of God today. What we call intercession is generally prayer, and quite honestly, a tremendous amount of it is self-centered prayer. It is not wrong. It is just that it is all to do with ourselves—all to do with our needs, all to do with our problems, and all to do with what we want from the Lord. There is nothing wrong with it. The word *prayer* means "pouring out"; and the Lord wants us to pour out. He loves us; He is Father to us. He wants us to pour out our hearts. But intercession is in another dimension. Intercession is not self-centered. Indeed, there can be no intercession unless a self-life is laid down. That is why there is so little intercession. And because there is so little intercession, there is stunted growth, superficiality, shallowness, the counterfeit, and the artificial among the people of God. There is every kind of obstacle and problem sitting almost upon the people of God and the work of God, because the people of God have never come to the position that God longs that they should occupy.

In the New Testament, of course, this whole matter is taken up as priests. We are priests; we speak of the priesthood of all believers. And of course we see it in terms of worship and in terms of praise, which is absolutely right. But intercession is a vital part of the ministry of a priest.

We see this in many of the great characters in the word of God. From our Jewish tradition, the great intercessors are Abraham, Moses, Samuel, and Daniel. In the Jewish tradition Daniel is not called a prophet although for most Christians he is the prophet *par excellence*. He is the one who speaks more about the future than any other prophet, who predicts things and yet in our tradition he is not called a prophet. He is called an intercessor. And it is very interesting that these four great characters all stand at the turning point in the fulfillment of God's purpose—Abraham, the beginning of the people of God, a chosen family; Moses, the beginning of a nation; Samuel, the beginning of a kingdom; Daniel, the restoration of something that could be lost. And in all these four great turning points in the purpose of God, we find that God has a man. We shall see many other kinds of lessons in the lives of these men, but every one of them was an intercessor. This perhaps more than anything else brings us face to face with the enormous importance of intercession.

We see this, of course, in our Lord Jesus. If we look at His high priestly prayer in John 17, we find another side to the Lord Jesus even while He was here on earth. In John 17:9, 12, 15, 20 we read, "I pray for them: I pray not for the world, but for those whom Thou hast given me; for they are Thine...While I was with them, I kept them in Thy name which thou hast given Me: and I guarded them, and not one of them perished, but the son of perdition; that the scripture might be fulfilled (intercession) ... I pray not that thou shouldest take them from the world, but that thou shouldest keep them from the evil one...Neither for these only do I pray, but for them also that believe on me through their word."

Here is intercession even with our Lord Jesus. We know He prayed. We know He withdrew from them at times, but here we have a glimpse into the intercessory ministry of the Lord Jesus, even in the midst of an unbelievably busy life and calling. Of course, we know that the Lord Jesus is engaged at this moment in this intercessory ministry, for we are told in the word of God in Hebrews 7:25–26: "Wherefore also He is able to save to the uttermost them that draw near unto God through him, seeing He ever liveth to make intercession for them."

And the apostle Paul tells us in Romans 8:34: "It is Christ Jesus that died, yea rather, that was raised from the dead, who is at the right hand of God, who also maketh intercession for us. Who shall separate us from the love of Christ"—with such an intercessor at the right hand of the Father?

If you and I do not know anything about intercession, I very much doubt we shall ever come to the throne of God. That is a dreadful thing to say for many people because they feel intercession is for an elite, pious, few who are of no earthly good. They are so mystical their heads are wrapped up in the clouds. They cannot wash a floor; they cannot bring up a baby; they cannot even control the dog. Because of this, we say they are so moony, so dreamy, they were born intercessors. But it is very interesting when you look at the intercessors in the Bible. All of them were unbelievably practical people. Moses was trained in Pharaoh's palace and was leading a nation. He was not some naturally dreamy, mystical type. He was quite the opposite. He was a very down-to-earth person, very practical in all his ways. And God finally brought him to be an intercessor.

Why do I say that you will never come to the throne of God if you do not become an intercessor? It is because intercession is the crown of all real ministry. And intercession requires a whole number of things that are related to coming to the throne of God. You have to lay down your life. You have to make a total commitment to the Lord. You have to learn how to discern the mind of God and the heart of God in given situations. Then you have to learn how to cooperate with the Lord, stand with the Lord, and see the fulfillment of His mind and heart's purpose in very troubled situations. This is intercession.

Moses is quite remarkable. He only became an intercessor when he laid down his life. Once he let go of his life he became an intercessor. There are many incidents of intercession in Moses' life. We read just one in Numbers, and Exodus 32 has another. Each time the Lord put him to the test. What was the Lord doing? The Lord was playing on everything that a man like Moses would love. He said to Moses: "Stand aside; I am fed up with these people. I am going to obliterate them."

I have no doubt at all that sometimes Moses felt the same. I have been long enough among the people of God to know that in leadership there are times when you wish the earth would open up and swallow them up or fire would come down from heaven and incinerate them. Praise the Lord, that does not last for too long normally, but you get so annoyed with the people of God. You get so irritated. Wasn't Moses the same kind of person? He was only a human being with a very strong personality and a very great character. I can believe that at times he could have wished with all his heart that he did not have to put up with this murmuring, critical, negative people, all dragging their feet, all talking about the onions and garlic and leeks of Egypt. Can you imagine it with a calling that Moses knew they had? Can you imagine it with the word of God that Moses had communicated to them? Can you imagine it with the tabernacle, the dwelling place of God? God wanted to dwell in the midst of this people and all they could think of was garlic, leeks, and onions.

I know many of you are not interested in garlic, leeks, and onions, but you might be interested in hot dogs or hamburgers or something else. But it is the same kind of thing. The point is they would exchange their inheritance and their birthright, their blessing for a mess of pottage, a stew. And the Lord played on Moses and said, "Moses, stand aside. I am going to obliterate them." It could have gotten a reaction in Moses, but then the Lord said something far more interesting: "I will make of *you* a great nation." Now if there was just a little bit of self-life in Moses he could have thought, "I think a thousand of me might be much easier to deal with than a thousand of them." Aren't we strange people? Can you imagine if the church was a thousand of me? We would have so many problems. Because we are such proud people, we want an empire. We want to be something. We want to have a name that will be everlasting. We want to be an integral part of the fulfillment of God's purpose. "Stand aside, Moses, I am going to destroy this people, but I will take you and make of you a great nation. My whole purpose will be centered in you, Moses, and will be fulfilled through you."

Do you really think the Lord meant it? The Lord never tests what cannot come through. If you have no trial in your life, it is because there is nothing worth testing. If you are having a joy ride, it is no commendation. It means there is so little of the Lord in your life He cannot put it to the test. The Lord proves what is real gold by testing, but He will only test when there is gold there to be tested.

What the Lord was really doing with Moses was simply saying to him, "I want to see whether you really have spiritual character." If there had been the slightest response and reaction on Moses' part: "Why, Lord, that is a good idea. I think You and I should sit down together on this matter. You know this lot; I do not think we are going to get anywhere with them." No! God had already revealed something to Moses. Remember? the thorn bush and the fire. It was as if God was saying, "Moses, this people is a thorn bush and I am in the midst of them. Now, did you get that lesson?"

Moses rose to it every time. Every time he called upon the Lord, he brought back the very declarations the Lord Himself had made. That is intercession. He took back to the Lord the very declarations that God Himself had made concerning Himself, concerning His character, concerning His purpose, and used that as the basis for his intercession. In one case he even said, "Lord, blot me out, but do not blot out this nation." He came as near to the character of the Lord Jesus as it was possible to come. This is intercession.

According to our tradition, Moses had a happy marriage but there were some irritants in it. And that is one of the reasons why, again according to our tradition, he married this black lady, this Cushite, a lady from Sudan. It caused a terrible storm in the family. Miriam and Aaron were older than Moses; Moses was the young one of the family. Think of that! Miriam had always looked after him. She was watching over him when he was a little baby in the ark. She never got over looking after her younger brother.

She always felt some big responsibility for him. So when he married that Cushite woman, the bottom fell out of her life. She could not believe that he had done such a thing. She went to Aaron and poured out her whole complaint to him, and Aaron fully shared her feeling. They felt that Moses had really let the family down, let everybody down, and so they had it out with him. All the bitterness came out into the open: "Do you think you are the only one God speaks to? He speaks to us, you know." And Miriam said, "Don't you remember that song I composed when we had passed over the Red Sea? We have all been used by the Lord, not just you, Moses. And now you have gone and done this thing. It is really terrible. You should repent." And the Lord heard the whole thing. The Lord came down and He was angry. Very interestingly, the Lord said, "I am going to take Miriam." And I imagine He meant Aaron as well. Aaron was so shocked, he turned to Moses and said, "Moses, plead with the Lord for Miriam, your sister."

And Moses prayed the shortest prayer we have of Moses in Scripture: "Lord, I beseech You, heal her." It was intercession again.

All I want you to see is that Moses came to the place where he was an intercessor. And as far as God is concerned, that meant even more to the Lord than his being the vehicle through which the word came and through which the tabernacle, the dwelling place was revealed. The intercessor is the bride. The very character of the bride is to lose herself for the Lord and for others.

The Need for Intercessors

Why are there so few intercessors? Why? The need is tremendous. We need intercessors for America. We need intercessors for men and women to be saved in this country. There is no hope for the United States unless the Spirit of God brings an awakening in American society and sweeps thousands of Americans into the kingdom of God. Apart from that there is no hope. There is a tremendous need for intercessors.

Then we need those who will pray for growth, not just salvation. Salvation is not so hard. It is getting people to grow up in the Lord instead of having all our fellowships filled with stunted babies, dwarfs, ugly. It is so ugly when a person has been saved for ten, twenty years, and they are not growing up in the Lord. When they are still a little dwarf, there is something ugly about it, something abnormal, something repellent. And yet we have to say the family of God is filled with babies.

One of the problems is that nobody understands the cry of the apostle Paul in Galatians 4:19: "My little children of whom I am again in travail [the agony of childbirth] until Christ be fully formed in you." He had been in travail for their salvation, now he was back in travail once more that Christ be fully formed in them. This is the ministry we need. It is unbelievable. Brothers in ministry can minister and minister and minister. We can give you the word and the word and the word, and still people do not grow. All they get is big in their heads. We need people who will become those so in fellowship with the Lord Jesus by the Spirit of God that they will pray into being men and women who are giants in the Lord spiritually, men and women who will grow in the Lord spiritually. If we do not have this intercession, the enemy will see to it that we have stunted, dwarfed abnormalities in the family of God.

It is not just a question of salvation or spiritual growth; it is a question of the church. The church will never be formed until there are those who lay down their lives. Until there is a spirit of intercession you will never see the church of God formed. You can get a collection of saints together and they will fall apart as quickly as they came together. It is a spiritual birth of the church that is required, and this can only come through intercession.

Take the work of the Lord. Oh, the need that there is all over the world in the work of the Lord!

Spiritual Maturity

What then are the requirements of the intercessor? We see it in Moses. First of all, a minimal, spiritual maturity. Travail—it is not for nothing that the Holy Spirit uses the word *travail*, the agony of childbirth. A babe cannot give birth; a kindergarten child cannot give birth. You have to have a certain minimal development and maturity to conceive and give birth. So it is in intercession. If you and I do not grow up in the Lord we cannot become intercessors. We see this in Moses. He could not be an intercessor in Egypt. He could not be an intercessor when he saw those two fighting. It was only after forty years in the desert that the condition was finally produced that could bring Moses to intercession.

I always quote a Chinese proverb here: "A journey of a thousand miles begins with one step." People listen to this and say, "I will never be an intercessor, that's clear. I am no good. I am immature. I am small. I am self-centered." Don't give up; take the first step.

The Lord is so short of intercessors that the moment you say, "Here I am," He will snap you up. Your education will start tonight. Your spiritual development, your being brought to spiritual maturity will begin almost immediately. The Lord so longs for candidates for intercession.

Total Commitment to the Lord

The second thing is this. There has to be a total commitment to the Lord, spirit, soul, and body. We often think of intercession as five minutes in the morning. That is not intercession; that is prayer. We sometimes think of intercession as half an hour in the day. It is not intercession; it is prayer. We sometimes think of intercession as one hour a week. That is not intercession; it is prayer. Intercession requires *you*, not your mouth. Intercession requires you. When the word of God tells us to pray without ceasing, what does it mean? Shall we all become nuns and monks shutting ourselves away in convents and monasteries? Is that what is meant? No. You can have the busiest life, you may be a successful businessman, a successful professional man, a successful housewife, a successful mother, but in your busy life, by committing yourself spirit, soul, and body to the Lord, you will become an intercessor. There will be within your spirit unceasing prayer.

The Self-life Laid Down

Third, there can be no intercession without a self-life laid down. If you hang on to that self-life there is no intercession. Oh, you can pray, you can praise, and you can inquire, but there is no intercession.

The Ministry of the Holy Spirit

Fourth, you must know the ministry of the Holy Spirit. "The Spirit Himself maketh intercession for us with groanings which cannot be uttered." Now I have seen some unbelievable things in this matter. The weirdest extravagances I have witnessed have been in this matter of groanings. I have been in meetings where I have heard people groaning and the pastor said to me, "Are you being disturbed by that noise?" I said, "Well, not disturbed but I wonder what it is all about." "Our brother has the ministry of groaning."

There was a meeting in Washington where a lady came up to me afterwards and said she had been to a prayer clinic. (I had schools of prayer but I had never heard of a prayer clinic. I thought: "Someone has a different name for a school of prayer.") So I asked her what she meant by a prayer clinic. She said, "I have been on a course." (This was in Florida.)

"How long was the course?"

"It was three months."

"Three months!" I said.

She said, "The first course was on how to know the Lord in prayer. But now I have just started my second course—groaning."

So I said to her, "Groaning, what do you mean?"

"Groaning—you know, like in Romans 8."

So I said, "Do you mean to tell me that someone teaches you how to groan?"

And she said to me, "Yes, that is right."

Aren't Americans incredible? Can you believe that there could be any people so naïve?

Then she said, "He tells me what to do, I do it, and then he corrects me."

Then suddenly, being Jewish, as the saying goes, "the penny dropped," and I said to her, "Are you paying for this course?" And she was—one hundred and fifty dollars for the course. Can you believe that? So stupid! No wonder the Lord calls His people sheep. You would have thought people would have the shrewdness, the astuteness, the spiritual awareness to realize there was something questionable here. I will give the lady one thing. She had a question about it. That is why she came to talk to me.

Brothers and sisters, there is a groaning, and it cannot be uttered. It is a pain within the spirit. It cannot be expressed in words and not even in many ways audibly. It is trapped within until it gets birthed; the time of birth comes. This is intercession. It is the Spirit of the Lord within us, in our spirit, conceiving burden, and as it were, not allowing us to escape.

Pressing on Toward the Goal

The second lesson from the life of Moses is pressing on toward the goal to the prize of the high calling of God. Moses is the most marvelous example of pressing on. It seems as if this dear servant of God, this man of God, this prophet of God, the more he saw of the Lord, the more he was inflamed to reach out toward the goal. The more he saw the Lord, the more he knew that he did not know. I find it very sad among the people of God that we have all these know-it-alls. These are people who have got it all in their heads. They can tell you everything, put you right on almost anything, and direct you on anything. They are know-it-alls. We used to have a hymn that has a line in it that I always quote in this connection. It was not meant to sound like this but it says, "And now I know it all." Actually it meant, "Now I know the love of God." It was very unfortunate it had that line in it. "Now I know it all."

Many believers give the impression of exactly that: "And now I know it all. I understand. I have had a second blessing; I know it all. I have had a baptism of the Spirit; I know it all. I have seen what God's purpose is; I know it all."

Is it not interesting that the more Moses saw the more he knew there was to see? Sometimes we think that if God revealed Himself to Moses in the burning bush that was it. There would be no more. Moses saw the Lord in the burning bush. He had the unmentionable and awesome name of God revealed to him, I AM THAT I AM, for the first time in history. He had the word of God communicated through him. He had the tabernacle, the dwelling place of God, the pattern of the two given to him, to communicate. You would have thought all this would represent a tremendous amount of knowing the Lord, of seeing the Lord. But here in Exodus 33, we have a window into the very spiritual character of this man of God, and what does he say? "Show me now Thy ways."

I would have said, "Moses, don't be stupid. How greedy can you be? The Lord has already shown you His ways. What about the thorn bush? What about the I AM THAT I AM? What about the word of God that He has given you? Don't you think that is enough? You have seen the ways of the Lord. What about the tabernacle? Isn't that even more amazing? Now you are at the very heart of God." But Moses said, "No, I want to see more. I do not feel I really know the Lord as I ought to know the Lord." Do you see what has happened? The more he has seen the Lord, the more he wants to see the Lord. The more he knows the Lord, the more he knows there is to know of the Lord.

Let me put it another way. The more he knows the Lord, the less he knows, related to what there is to know. Many Christian's god is virtually an idol. He can only think what they think, he can only say what they say, and he can only do what they let him do. He is the projection of their own minds. But when you have seen the living God, you will never be the same again. When with the eyes of your heart you see the Lord, you will never be the same again.

Moses saw the mighty acts of the Lord. People get so excited about the mighty acts of the Lord—signs and wonders and miracles. I am all for them; the more the better. I cannot understand all these people who continuously devalue anything like that, as if it were nothing. Of course it is not nothing; it is a mighty act of God. It is one that God has done; you cannot call that nothing. How can you despise anything that God does? But these Christians are so superior and very elitist, downing that company—"All they are bothered about is signs and wonders." I am all for them. I wish there were a few more real signs and wonders here in North America. Maybe that would blow up the whole of society and start a whole attraction toward the Lord.

Hunger and Thirst for the Lord

But Moses had seen all these mighty acts, these wonders, these signs, and now, after Egypt, after the ten plagues, after the exodus, after the water out of the rock, after the manna, he says in this amazing way, "Show me now thy ways." Don't you think that is amazing?

The Lord said, "Very well, I will do this. I have granted you this thing. I am going to meet you. I am going to give you deeper understanding, Moses." I think it must be because he is Jewish. I cannot think of any other thing. He will not let the Lord go. "No, now I want to see Your glory." It was not for himself.

Listen carefully. Hunger and thirst are the greatest blessings that God could ever give you. Complacency is the greatest curse that can ever come into your life. Laodiceanism is complacency. "We have got it all; we are rich; we see; we have faith; we know." And the Lord says, "You do not know. You are blind. You are naked. You are poor." Complacency is a curse. Hunger is a blessing. "Blessed are those who hunger and thirst after righteousness for they shall be filled."

Here we see this hunger in Moses. The more he sees the Lord, the greater his hunger. The more he knows the Lord, the greater his thirst.

We see the same thing in the apostle Paul. I could never understand the testimony of the apostle Paul in Philippians 3, when he says he counts all things but loss that he might know Him. Well, I would have said, "Paul, what are you talking about? You have written the Roman letter, I and II Corinthians, the Galatians letter, the letter to Philemon. There are even one or two other letters you have written, and yet you say you do not know the Lord. I do not understand it."

"I have not already obtained." You have not already obtained? Where does that leave me? He had even been caught up to the third heaven and heard things which are not lawful for a man to utter. Think of that! Most of us would be going around the platforms of the world billed as: WHAT I HEARD IN THE THIRD HEAVEN.

Or at least we would write a few books on the subject. But here is the apostle who had been caught up to the third heaven, who had visions and understanding, and he was not even allowed to tell us what he saw. And now he says, "I have not already obtained." What is wrong with the man? If I had written, by the Spirit of God, I Corinthians 12, I would be so happy. If I had written I Corinthians 14, or 15, the great resurrection chapter, I would be so happy. Or maybe II Corinthians 4: "We have this treasure in earthen vessels." When we are in the glory, I would come to you and say, "Did you ever study what the Lord used me to write?" Oh, I would have been so thrilled.

Suppose the Lord had used me to write I Corinthians 13. But the apostle Paul was used by the Spirit of God to write the whole of the first Corinthian letter, the second Corinthian letter, and the Roman letter. And he says, "Not that I have already obtained." What does he mean? Where does it leave me? If the apostle feels that he has not yet obtained, he is not already made complete, what about me? Now we learn something. The apostle Paul, like Moses, is blessed with an insatiable hunger. It is a blessing. He has a hunger for the Lord and a thirst for the Lord, and the more he knows the Lord, the more he sees the Lord, the more he knows there is to know of the Lord and to see of the Lord.

How much we need this! We are so complacent. We are so self-satisfied. We feel as long as we can understand a little here, a little there, that is it. May the Lord get us on our knees, crying out to Him to give us a hunger. When a person develops a hunger for God, things begin to happen because the Lord says, "Blessed are those who hunger and thirst after righteousness for they shall be filled." Those that seek Him surely find Him.

Moses Made Perfect in Love

The third lesson is: Moses made perfect in love. There is a false but generally held view about Moses which I think is a terrible slander on his character. It goes like this. Moses is a legalist. He is a stark, stern, distant, impersonal servant of God. He represents the Law; there is no love. There may be a little bit of truth in it. Maybe Moses, the strong man that he was, found it very hard in the beginning to use the vocabulary of love. It is surely quite remarkable that he hardly uses the word *love* in Exodus, Leviticus, and Numbers.

I think you all remember how Mr. Sparks pronounced Deuteronomy. He always said, "Deuteronomy," because it means the second Law-giving. Think for a moment. (The problem with most of us is that we do not think.) Why did the Lord repeat the giving of the Law? Isn't it strange? Does the Lord just like repeating things? Why didn't He just say in a sentence: "Go back to Exodus and study carefully the Law"? Why did He give the Law all over again?

Deuteronomy is to Genesis, Exodus, Leviticus, and Numbers what the gospel of John is to Matthew, Mark, and Luke. John is an interpretation and adds something that is not so apparent in the first three gospels. Deuteronomy actually does the same for those first four books. Now here is the most amazing thing. For the first time Moses uses the word *love*. This is what he says in Deuteronomy 6:4: "Hear O Israel: the Lord our God is one Lord:

and thou shalt love the Lord thy God with all thy heart, and with all thy soul, and with all thy might."

Deuteronomy 7:6–9: "For thou art a holy people unto the Lord thy God: the Lord thy God hath chosen thee to be a people for His own possession, above all peoples that are upon the face of the earth. The Lord did not set His love upon you, nor choose you, because ye were more in number than any people; for ye were the fewest of all peoples: but because the Lord loveth you, (You will not find this in Exodus.) and because He would keep the oath which he sware unto your fathers, hath the Lord brought you out with a mighty hand, and redeemed you out of the house of bondage, from the hand of Pharaoh king of Egypt. Know therefore that the Lord thy God, He is God, the faithful God, who keepeth covenant and lovingkindness with them that love Him and keep His commandments to a thousand generations."

This word *lovingkindness* in the Revised Standard is "steadfast love" in some of the modern versions. In the old King James it is "mercy." In Hebrew it is the word *chesed* that you cannot put really into English. It means "the faithful love of a husband to a wife." It is covenanted love. It is loyal love. It has mercy in it because it is from someone much greater to someone much less. I cannot explain it. But everywhere through the word of God you have *chesed*. When they went out to battle, what did they sing? "The *chesed* of the Lord endures forever."

Deuteronomy 10:12–13a, 15: "And now, Israel, what doth the Lord thy God require of thee, but to fear the Lord thy God, to walk in all His ways, and to love Him, and to serve the Lord thy God with all thy heart and with all thy soul, to keep the commandments of the Lord...Only the Lord had a delight in thy fathers to love them, and He chose their seed after them, even you above all peoples, as at this day."

There is a new element in this whole thing. This is the second giving of the Law, only it is given in a new light. It is love, love, love. It is the love of God.

What I want to remind you is what the Lord Jesus said. A godly scribe came to Jesus, and because he had noted the way Jesus answered, he said, "What is the greatest commandment?" Mark gives this in its proper Jewish form. The Lord Jesus said, "Hear, O Israel, The Lord our God, the Lord is one: and thou shall love the Lord thy God with all thy heart, and with all thy soul, and with all thy mind, and with all thy strength. The second is this, Thou shall love thy neighbor as thyself" (Mark 12:29–31).

In Matthew's Gospel he adds this word: "Upon these two hang the whole law and prophets." In other words, the Lord Jesus was saying what we find in Galatians. It is fulfilling the royal law of love.

Moses was an unbelievably strong man, this man whom God had reduced to a dead, dry thorn bush so that he might know the Lord. And now we find the love of God is made perfect in him. What does it mean when John says three or four times in his letter: "The love of God made perfect"? He says that God's love may be made perfect. In another place he says that you may be perfected in love. I think that this is one of the great lessons of Moses' life. If the Lord Jesus summed up everything by "Thou shall love the Lord thy God with all thy strength, with all thy soul, with all thy might, and thou shall love thy neighbor as thyself," does that not bring within it a challenge to us? Is my service out of love for the Lord? Is my fellowship out of love for my brothers and sisters?

The apostle Paul, who in many ways is the New Testament parallel to Moses, when he writes that amazing first letter to the Corinthians and talks about the church, the functioning of the church, the meetings, and the building up, he says, "And moreover a most excellent way show I unto you. If I speak with the tongues of men and of angels, but have not love, I am become sounding brass, or a clanging cymbal. And if I have the gift of prophecy, and know all mysteries and all knowledge (I think of Moses.); and if I have all faith, so as to remove mountains (I think of Moses.), but have not love, I am nothing. And if I bestow all my goods to feed the poor, and if I give my body to be burned, but have not love, it profiteth me nothing. Love suffereth long, and is kind; love envieth not; love vaunteth not itself, is not puffed up, doth not behave itself unseemly, seeketh not its own, is not provoked, taketh not account of evil; rejoiceth not in unrighteousness, but rejoiceth with the truth; beareth all things, believeth all things, hopeth all things, endureth all things. Love never faileth" (I Corinthians 12:31b–13:8a).

It is a wonderful thing to see in Moses that at the end he came to this. And in the second giving of the Law we have a new note. We discover that behind the whole thing is the love of God, and because the love of God is behind it, love being love requires love, calls for love, looks for love.

Is it not an interesting thing that the Ephesian church, which was so marvelous and commended by the Lord in many ways, yet still He would remove the lampstand from its place for one reason only: they had left their first love. Here then is the third lesson from the life of Moses. It is all to do with spiritual character. There is no such thing as spiritual character without love. And there is no such thing as genuine service without love.

Moses Finished the Course

The last lesson is that Moses finished the course God set before him. Have you noticed how many people begin in the spirit and end in the flesh? Have you noticed how so many people who are born of God never reach God's end? Moses finished the course. Like the apostle Paul he could say, "I fought the good fight, I finished the course, I have kept the faith" (II Timothy 4:7).

Moses had brought the people right out of Egypt, right through the wilderness, and right to the edge of the Promised Land. Moses had communicated to them the word of God, which would be absolutely foundational and fundamental to the people of God forever afterwards. Moses had given them the pattern of the truth, the tabernacle, the dwelling place of God. In other words, it was an understanding, if only in embryonic form, of the heart of God and the desire of God to have a home in the spirit. All of this Moses had fulfilled. Now he comes to the end.

Moses Died

There is yet another fallacy about Moses that I would like just to mention. I do not know where it came from, but there is an idea that Moses never died. And because of this some divines have suggested that the two witnesses at the end of the earth are Elijah and Moses. Isn't this amazing! Simply because they could not find his sepulcher, they said he did not really die. And yet the Lord said, "Go up on Mount Nebo because you are going to die and be gathered to your people." Furthermore, in the New Testament it shows you. In Jude it says the archangel Michael did not dare to bring a railing accusation against Satan when Satan was contending for the dead body of Moses. So it is very clear that he had died. The Muslims have a tomb for him not far from Jerusalem which none of us recognize.

Moses died, and if the Lord tarries we are all going to go. I do not mean to be depressing; I think it is very wonderful. There is a very strange Hebrew construction here. It says, "And Moses died according to the word of God." But in the Hebrew it literally says, "Moses died on the mouth of God." And this is why the Rabbis said, "God kissed him and he died." The Rabbis said that God loved Moses so much and Moses meant so much to Him even though he was denied going over into the land because of that one disobedience. And he was forever an example to all of us that we have to obey the Lord. We have to remember that God's people are an old thorn bush in which the flame of fire burns. Still there was such joy in the heart of God—Moses reached the goal. Moses did get into the land because he was there with the Lord Jesus on Mount Tabor or Mount Hermon, whichever you like, at the transfiguration.

God Buried Moses

But there is another very wonderful thing. Again in the Hebrew it says, "And He buried him." They changed it in some of the modern versions because they feel that God could not have buried him. So they put, "They buried him." But the Hebrew says, "And He buried him." That is why we do not have a tomb; God took him and buried him. And that is why Satan realized even the dead body of Moses was so precious to God, he wanted to try and get it. Can you believe that! Some Christians do not have any time for their body. They say that when they are dead they do not care what happens to it. Don't talk like that. Your body is very precious. Even that body with sin in its members is very precious. When we bury it, it is an act of faith because from the atoms of your disintegrating body you will be raised with a resurrection body. Isn't that marvelous! When you are getting older, it is marvelous. When you are young, you don't feel like this. But when you are old and you have aches and pains and the sight is going, the teeth are dropping out, wrinkles are coming, and hair is falling out, what a wonderful thing it is to think we are going to have a body like His. Here is a finished course.

Are you going to finish the course? Well, you will never finish it in your own strength. You will need all the grace of the Lord and all the power of the Holy Spirit to finish this course, but the grace of the Lord is available to you. The power of the Holy Spirit is available to you. There is no reason why you should not finish the course, keep the faith, having fought the good fight. No reason at all!

The Lord Jesus in a parable spoke of the Father saying, "Well done, good and faithful servant." Isn't that another way to say, "The Lord kissed him"? "Well done." "The Lord took him." Don't be afraid about your going. If you have lived faithfully with the Lord and walked faithfully with the Lord, laid down your life, your end will be exactly as the Lord determines it. All the grace of God will be there, and all the angels you need to help you through that last point into the presence of God. Never fear. We hope that we do not have to die. We hope that the Lord will descend with a shout, with the trump of God. Think of it! In the twinkling of an eye—have you ever seen an eye twinkle? In the twinkling of an eye we shall all be changed. Whether we die or whether we live nobody is going to get there first. The dead in Christ, it is true, will rise first, and then we who are alive and remain will be caught up together. We will all be together. It will all happen within a moment in time. Moses finished his course.

Here is the last lesson of Moses' life. What a wonderful thing it would be with all our failings, all our weaknesses, and with all our tendency to sin, to say by the grace of God and the power of the Holy Spirit that the Lord Himself will step into our last moments and take us. There is nothing to fear with the Lord. No wonder dear Moses said, "The eternal God is thy refuge and underneath are the everlasting arms."

Shall we pray:

Lord, we need You and we want to just commit ourselves to You. We have had such a lovely time around Your table and now Lord, all we want to ask is that You will take this word of Yours and write it on our hearts. There are all kinds of things you can bring back to us by Your Spirit in the days that lie ahead. We want to be intercessors, Lord. Help us to take the first step. Help us to surrender to You, Lord. We want to be those who press on toward the goal for the prize of the high calling that You have in the Lord Jesus.

Oh Father, bless us with hunger and thirst; a hunger and a thirst for Yourself that will never be satisfied. Always we want more of You, more of You, more of You. Lord, bless us with such hunger and such thirst. Lord, You have loved us. You have loved us with an everlasting love and drawn us with the cords of love. You have set Your love on us.

Forgive us that we love so little. Forgive us for the poverty of our love, Lord, for the coldness of our response. Lord, inflame us with Your Love. Let that flame of fire in this thorn bush be the flame of eternal love. Do it, Lord, for Your namesake, we pray. And may in all of us Your love be made perfect.

And Lord, help us to finish the course. You have made all the grace available and all the power available. Help us to finish the course, that at the end of it we shall find You waiting, arms outstretched with that "well done." Lord, hear us. We ask it in the name of our Lord Jesus. Amen.

Other books by Lance Lambert

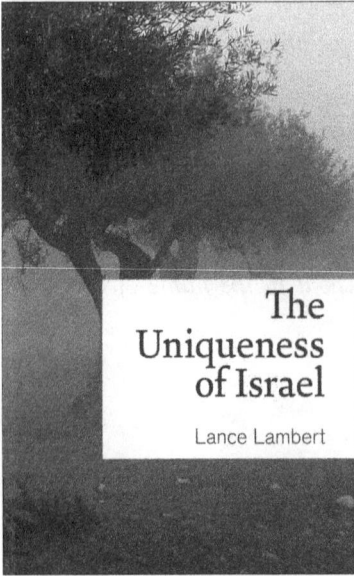

The Uniqueness of Israel

Woven into the fabric of Jewish existence there is an undeniable uniqueness. There is bitter controversy over the subject of Israel, but time itself will establish the truth about this nation's place in God's plan. For Lance Lambert, the Lord Jesus is the key that unlocks Jewish history He is the key not only to their fall, but also to their restoration. For in spite of the fact that they rejected Him, He has not rejected them.

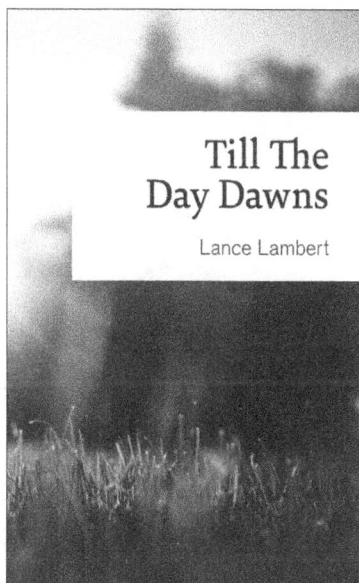

Till the Day Dawns

"And we have the word of prophecy made more sure; whereunto ye do well that ye take heed, as unto a lamp shining in a dark place, until the day dawn, and the day-star arise in your hearts." (II Peter 1:9).

The word of prophecy was not given that we might merely be comforted but that we would be prepared and made ready. Let us look into the Word of God together, searching out the prophecies, that the Day-Star arise in our hearts until the Day dawns.

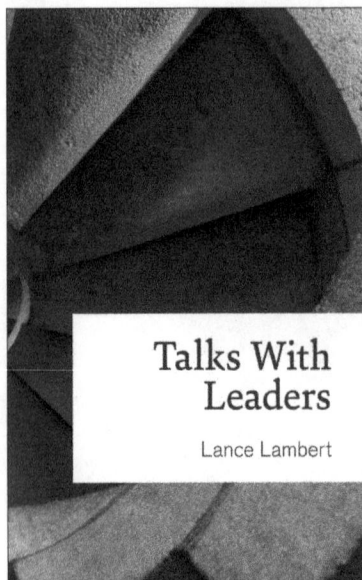

Talks With
Leaders

Lance Lambert

Talks With Leaders

"O Timothy, guard that which is committed unto thee ..."
(1 Timothy 6:20) Has God given you something? Has God
deposited something in you? Is there something of Himself
which He has given to you to contribute to the people of God?
Guard it. Guard that vision which He has given you. Guard that
understanding that He has so mercifully granted to you. Guard
that experience which He has given that it does not evaporate or
drain away or become a cause of pride. Guard that which the Lord
has given to you by the Holy Spirit. In these heart-to-heart talks
with leaders Lance Lambert covers such topics as the character
of God's servants, the way to serve, the importance of anointing,
and hearing God's voice. Let us consider together how to remain
faithful with what has been entrusted to us.

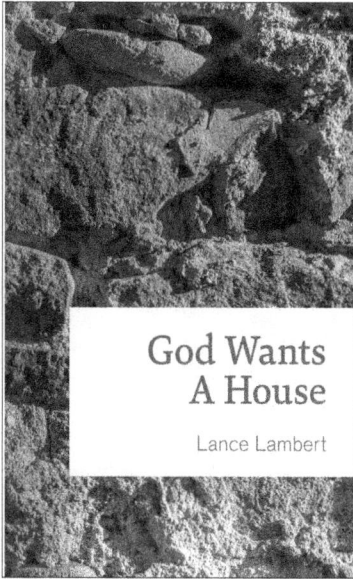

God Wants
A House

Lance Lambert

God Wants a House

Where is God at home? Is He at home in Richmond, VA? Is He
at home in Washington? Is He at home in Richmond, Surrey? Is
He at home in these other places? Where is God at home? There
are thousands of living stones, many, many dear believers with
real experience of the Lord, but where has the ark come home?
Where are the staves being lengthened that God has finally come
home? In God Wants a House Lance looks into this desire of the
Lord, this desire He has to dwell with His people. What would
this dwelling look like? Let's seek the Lord, that we can say with
David, "One thing have I asked of Jehovah, that will I seek after:
that I may dwell in the house of Jehovah all the days of my life, To
behold the beauty of Jehovah, And to inquire in his temple."